KETOGENIC DIET 200
RECIPES
Reclaim Your Waist, Burn Fat & Shed Pounds Really Fast And Easy

By Jennifer Wittman

Table of Contents

Introduction

I want to thank you and congratulate you for downloading the book, ***"Ketogenic Diet 200 Recipes. Reclaim Your Waist, Burn Fat & Shed Pounds Really Fast And Easy"***.

This book of recipes is packed with a wealth of tips and tricks regarding how to implement the Ketogenic diet in the interest of quick and efficient weight loss, as well as health strategies.

The ketogenic diet, sometimes referred to as the "keto" diet is a method that was created to induce your body to make ketones, which is a byproduct of when there is not enough glucose to use for energy. They are a product of the liver breaking down fat. Ketones can be considered an alternative to carbohydrates, which enables your body to fuel itself on fat alone, allowing you to burn fat effectively in the process. This form of metabolism, called ketosis, is a perfectly natural process of the body, and has been used by many people for its known benefits in weight loss.

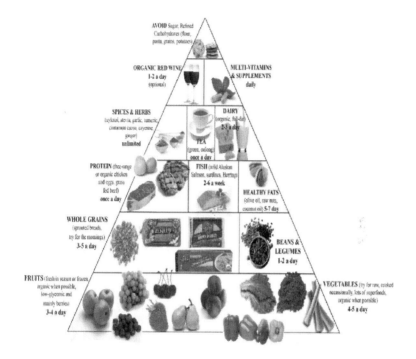

AVOID Sugar, Refined Carbohydrates (flour, pasta, grains, potatoes)

ORGANIC RED WINE
1-2 a day
(optional)

MULTI-VITAMINS
& SUPPLEMENTS
daily

SPICES & HERBS
(xylitol, stevia, garlic, tumeric, cinnamon cacao, cayenne, ginger)
unlimited

DAIRY
(organic, full-fat)
2-3 a day

TEA
(green, oolong)
once a day

PROTEIN (free-range or organic chicken and eggs, grass fed beef)
once a day

FISH (wild Alaskan Salmon, sardines, Herring)
2-6 a week

HEALTHY FATS
(olive oil, raw nuts, coconut oil) 5-7 day

WHOLE GRAINS
(sprouted breads, try for the morning)
3-5 a day

BEANS & LEGUMES
1-2 a day

FRUITS (fresh in season or frozen, organic when possible, low-glycemic and mainly berries)
3-4 a day

VEGETABLES (try for raw, cooked occasionally, lots of superfoods, organic when possible)
4-5 a day

Chapter 1 How does the keto diet work?

To induce your body's natural state of ketosis, you'll have to ensure that a large portion of your caloric intake for the day is sourced from fat. Around 70 to 80 percent should do it, and make up the remaining 10-30% with a mixture of carbs and protein.

You'll want to limit your carbohydrate intake the most – around 35 grams a day should be your limit. For reference, an apple, glass of milk or a slice of bread should fit the bill. Once you've done this, your body should be able to adapt itself and change to use ketones as a primary energy source instead.

This adaptation process is somewhat slow however, which can be anywhere from 2-7 days, and the speed of adaptation depends on your individual activity level, body type as well as the foods you're taking in. You may also check to see if your body is in a ketosis state through clinical tests including blood, urine and breath tests.

Foods To Eat On The Keto Diet

Ketosis is reached by eating a large amount of fat compared to carbohydrates in your daily intake. By reducing your carbohydrate intake even further, you can push your body to produce more ketones more efficiently. Although counterintuitive, it may be wise to avoid fruits – especially extra sweet sorts – since they can easily tick over your carb limit for the day and throw off your body's adapting ketosis state.

Ketogenic diets should be roughly composed of 5% carbohydrates, 25% protein and 70% fat. Your day-to-day foods should a majority of the time consist of:

- **Protein**: Chicken, oral and organ meat, duck, bacon, nut butters, steak, sausage, ground beef, ham and pork chops.

- **Fats and oils:** Avocado, coconut oil, egg yolks, butter, shellfish, olive oil and fatty fish such like salmon and tuna.

- **Vegetables:** Veggies that grow above ground in which green and leafy choices are preferable.

Dairy can be added occasionally to the ketogenic diet, which can become another good source of fats that you can eat. Be cautious, however, as if you overeat dairy products, you may end up eating more than your recommended intake of carbohydrates. Hard cheeses and full-fat soft cheeses, along with heavy whipped cream and greek yoghurt are great dairy choices to be eating whilst on the ketogenic diet.

Instead of conventional sugars, try natural sweeteners such as sucralose, stevia and erythritol as alternatives if you must have something sweetened.

Foods to avoid on the keto diet

Carbohydrates, as mentioned before, take up only 5% of your recommended daily intake whilst on the ketogenic diet. In saying so, any foods that have a high carb content should be avoided whilst in a state of ketosis. These include:

- *Low-fat foods:* Oftentimes, food that is low in fat has the flip-side of being high in sugar to compensate. Take caution when selecting these choices and be wary of food labels. Always check the nutritional information on such products if you're not convinced.

- *Fruit:* Large fruits in particular are known to have large quantities of simple sugars and carbohydrates. Berries on the other hand are okay to be eaten within reason.

- *Grains:* Wheat-based products are, by nature, carbohydrate loaded. Be careful around pasta, cakes, bread, cereals, rice, pastries, beer and corn and products that contain these.

- *Sugar:* Be careful and avoid all foods, especially processed ones that contain a large amount of sugar – especially added sugar. Chocolates, lollies and soft drinks are notoriously full of sugars that are often invisible at first glance.

- *Starch:* Oats, museli, yams, and potatoes are all starch-based foods that can add to your carbohydrate balance.

Chapter 2 KETOGENIC BREAKFAST

Bacon and Egg

Ingredients:

12 rashers bacon

½ cup of cream

12 eggs

2 cups of steamed broccoli

½ strong grated Cheddar

Seasoning to taste

Directions

Preheat oven to 350° F.

Grease a 12-cup muffin pan or 12 ramekins

Fry bacon until just before it crisps, and then use each rasher to line a compartment of the pan/ramekin.

Wisk together the other ingredients until well combined and divide equally amongst the pan compartments/ramekins.

Bake for around 20 minutes and serve.

Delicious Scrambled Eggs

Ingredients:

½ cup of cream

Seasoning to taste

A teaspoon of coconut oil/butter

½ cup of diced onion

½ cup of diced ham

½ cup of diced peppers

1 cup of mature cheddar (grated)

1 pinch of chili flakes (optional)

Directions

Beat the eggs, cream, and seasoning together.

Warm up a frying pan over medium heat. Add in the eggs, stirring so that the eggs scramble.

Add the rest of the ingredients, except the cheese.

Add the cheese when almost done and serve immediately.

Bacon-Cheddar Eggs Breakfast

Ingredients

12 hard-cooked eggs

1/2 cup mayonnaise

4 bacon strips, cooked and crumbled

2 tablespoons finely shredded Cheddar cheese

1 tablespoon honey mustard

1/4 teaspoon pepper

Directions

Slice eggs in half lengthwise; remove yolks and set whites aside.

In a small bowl, mash yolks.

Stir in the mayonnaise, bacon, cheese, mustard and pepper. Stuff into egg whites.

Refrigerate until serving.

Spinach Greek Frittata

Ingredients:

- 3 tablespoons Olive oil
- 10 eggs
- 5-ounce baby spinach
- 1-pint grape tomatoes, sliced
- 4 scallions, sliced
- 8-ounce feta, crushed
- 1-2 teaspoons salt
- ½ teaspoon fresh and ground pepper
- *Optional*: ¼ cup pitless Greek black olives

Directions:

1. Preheat the oven to 350° F and add oil in a casserole. Keep it in the oven for 5 minutes.

2. Whisk eggs, pepper, and salt together.

3. Add the following in order; tomatoes, scallions, spinach and feta.

4. Take out the casserole from the oven.

5. Transfer mixture to casserole and bake it for 25 to 30 minutes to get puffed and golden in color.

Garlic Scrambled Eggs with Sauce

Ingredients

2 eggs

1 leek, chopped

1 tablespoon vegetable oil

1 clove garlic, minced

3 tablespoons tomato sauce

Directions

In a small bowl, stir together eggs and chopped leek.

Heat the oil in a small skillet over medium heat. Add the egg mixture and cook until set.

Return skillet to heat and add garlic.

Saute garlic briefly then add tomato sauce. Pour warm sauce over eggs and serve.

Tasty Zucchini and Eggs

Ingredients

2 teaspoons olive oil

1 zucchini, sliced

1 egg, beaten

Salt and pepper to taste

Directions

Heat a small skillet over medium heat.

Pour in oil and saute zucchini until tender.

Spread out zucchini in an even layer, and pour beaten egg evenly over top. Cook until egg is firm.

Season with salt and pepper to taste.

Almond Savory Muffins

Ingredients:

1 cup of sour cream

2 cups of finely ground almond flour

2 free range eggs

1/16 cup of melted farm butter

½ teaspoon of thyme (dried)

½ teaspoon of baking soda

½ cup of mozzarella

½ cup of mature cheddar

Pinch of salt

Directions:

Set your oven at 400°F.

Mix all of the dry ingredients together and set to one side. In a different bowl, beat the eggs and the mix in the butter and sour cream. Mix both mixtures together until incorporated.

Stir in the cheeses and pour into a greased, six compartment muffin tray, ensuring that you divide the batter evenly.

Bake for about 15 minutes or until the muffins are lightly golden and cooked all the way through.

Double Cream Quiche

Ingredients:

6 cups of shredded cheddar

2 cups of double cream

1 finely chopped onion

Butter to fry onion in

12 free range eggs

2 teaspoons of dried thyme

1 teaspoon of salt

Directions:

Set your oven at 350°F.

Heat the butter up in a suitably sized frying pan and cook the onions until translucent. Leave to cool.

Grease two pie dishes or baking dishes. Layer the bottom of each with a third of the cheese. Divide the cooked onions between the two dishes.

Using a clean bowl, whisk the cream, eggs, and spices until completely incorporated. Add in the remaining cheese, and divide the mixture between the two baking dishes.

Bake for around 25 minutes or until the quiche has begun to go golden and is completely set.

Cauliflower Bacon Hash

Ingredients:

6 rashers of bacon

1 diced onion

2 cups of diced cauliflower

2 crushed cloves of garlic

Seasoning to taste

Directions:

Fry bacon until crisp and set aside to cool.

Chop into bite sized bits.

Using the same pan, mix in the rest of the ingredients and fry over medium heat for a few minutes until it browns.

Add bacon just before serving.

Keto Ham Breakfast

Ingredients:

12 eggs

4 cups of diced broccoli

2 cups of diced ham

½ cup each of mozzarella and grated cheddar cheese

Directions

Preheat the oven to 375° F.

Lightly blanch broccoli for about 3 minutes in boiling water.

Wisk the eggs and add cheese, ham, and broccoli

Pour into a suitable oven-proof dish and leave to cook for around half an hour.

Easy Rasher Bacon Breakfast

Ingredients:

6 eggs

4 rashers of bacon

½ cup of cream

Seasoning to taste

Directions:

Lightly fry bacon until crisp. Set aside and dice when cool.

Wisk together eggs, cream, and seasoning and scramble in the bacon fat.

Add bacon and serve.

Keto Pizza Frittata

Ingredients:

12 large Eggs

9oz. bag Frozen Spinach

1 oz. Pepperoni

5 oz. Mozzarella Cheese

1 tsp. Minced Garlic

1/2 cup Fresh Ricotta Cheese

1/2 cup Parmesan Cheese

4 tbsp. Olive Oil

1/4 tsp. Nutmeg

Salt and Pepper to Taste

Directions:

1. Microwave frozen spinach for about 3-4 minutes, or until defrosted (but not hot). Squeeze the spinach with your hands and drain of as much water as you can. Set aside.

2. Pre-heat oven to 375F. Mix together all of the eggs, olive oil, and spices. Whisk well until everything is combined.

3. Add in the ricotta cheese, parmesan cheese, and spinach. When adding the spinach, break it apart into small pieces with your hands.

4. Pour the mixture into a cast iron skillet, then sprinkle mozzarella cheese over the top. Add pepperoni on top of that.

5. Bake for 30 minutes. If you're using a glass container (instead of a cast iron), bake for 40-45 minutes or until completely set.

6. Slice and enjoy! Top with creme fraiche, ranch dressing, or your favorite fatty sauce on top if you'd like.

Low Carb Sausage Casserole

Ingredients:

1 cup Almond Flour

1/4 cup Flaxseed Meal

1 lb. Breakfast Sausage

10 large Eggs

4 oz. Cheddar Cheese

6 tbsp. Walden Farms Maple Syrup

4 tbsp. Butter

1/2 tsp. Onion Powder

1/2 tsp. Garlic Powder

1/4 tsp. Sage

Salt and Pepper to Taste

Directions:

1. Pre-heat oven to 350F. Put a pan on the stove over medium heat, then add the breakfast sausage.

2. As it cooks, break up with a wooden spoon and continue to cook until browned.

2. In a separate bowl, measure out all dry ingredients, then add the wet ingredients. Only add 4 tbsp. of the Walden Farm's Syrup, as we'll be using the other 2 tbsp. to top everything off. Mix together well.

3. Add in the cheese to the mixture and continue mixing again.

4. Once the sausage is browned and somewhat crispy, add everything (including excess fat) into the mixture for the casserole. Mix together well again.

5. Line a 9×9 casserole dish with parchment paper and then pour the casserole mixture into the dish. Use 2 tbsp. Walden Farm's Syrup drizzled over the top for extra maple flavor. You can use practically any larger casserole dish you'd like too (as it's rather thick). Just reduce the cooking time slightly if you are using a larger dish.

6. Place in the oven and bake for 45-55 minutes. You want the inside to be completely cooked through.

7. Once done, remove from the oven and let cool. Remove the casserole by holding on to the edges of the parchment paper and lifting out.

8. Slice and serve. Feel free to drizzle a little bit more syrup over each one, or serve with a little bit of Reduced Sugar Ketchup. Enjoy!

Flavour Keto Brownie Muffins

Ingredients:

1 cup Golden Flaxseed Meal

1/4 cup Cocoa Powder

1 tbsp. Cinnamon

1/2 tbsp. Baking Powder

1/2 tsp. Salt

1 large Egg

2 tbsp. Coconut Oil

1/4 cup Sugar-free Caramel Syrup

1/2 cup Pumpkin Puree

1 tsp. Vanilla Extract

1 tsp. Apple Cider Vinegar

1/4 cup Slivered Almonds

Directions:

1. Preheat your oven to 350°F and combine all your dry ingredients in a deep mixing bowl and mix to combine.

2. In a separate bowl, combine all your wet ingredients.

3. Pour your wet ingredients into your dry ingredients and mix very well to combine.

4. Line a muffin tin with paper liners and spoon about ¼ cup of batter into each muffin liner. This recipe should yield 6 muffins. Then sprinkle slivered almonds over the top of each muffin and press gently so that they adhere.

5. Bake in the oven for about 15 minutes. You should see the muffins rise and set on top. Enjoy warm or cool!

Avocado Cheesy Breakfast Tacos

Ingredients:

1 cup Mozzarella Cheese, shredded

6 large Eggs

2 tbsp. Butter

3 strips Bacon

1/2 small Avocado

1 oz. Cheddar Cheese, shredded

Salt and Pepper to Taste

Directions:

1. Start off by cooking the bacon. Line a baking sheet with foil and bake 3 strips in an oven for about 15-20 minutes at 375F.

2. While the bacon is cooking, heat 1/3 cup of mozzarella at a time on clean pan on medium heat. This cheese will form our taco shells.

3. Wait until the cheese is browned on the edges (about 2-3 minutes). Slide a spatula under it to unstick it. This should happen easily if you're using whole milk mozzarella as the oil from the cheese will prevent it from sticking.

4. Use a pair of tongs to lift the shell up and drape it over a wooden spoon resting on a pot. Do the same with the rest of your cheese, working in batches of 1/3 cups.

5. Next, cook your eggs in the butter, stirring occasionally until they're done. Season with salt and pepper.

6. Spoon a third of your scrambled eggs into each hardened taco shell.

7. Then add sliced avocado on top.

8. Follow this by adding the bacon (either chopped or whole strips).

9. Lastly, sprinkle cheddar cheese over the tops of the breakfast tacos. Add hot sauce and cilantro if you'd like and enjoy!

Parmesan Basil Omelet

Ingredients:

4 large eggs

1½ tablespoons freshly-chopped basil leaves

¾ cup grated parmesan cheese

2 thin slices of cooked ham, minced

1 small avocado, pitted and sliced

2 tablespoons coconut oil

Pinch of sea salt

Directions:

Whisk together the eggs and parmesan cheese. Add in the basil, ham and sea salt. Mix well.

Heat the coconut oil in a pan over medium-high flame. Once the oil is hot, pour in the egg mixture and cook for 30 seconds. To prevent the egg from burning, use a spatula to push the sides of the egg towards the center.

Flip the omelet and cook the other side for 1 minute. Once the omelet is cooked, remove it from the heat and transfer it to a serving plate.

Top the omelet with avocado slices and serve.

Cauliflower Bacon Breakfast Mash

Ingredients:

6 rashers of bacon

2 cups of cubed cauliflower

1 cubed onion

2 cloves of freshly ground garlic

Season to taste

½ teaspoon of powdered garlic

Directions:

Fry bacon till nice and crisp. Set aside to cool and crumble.

Using the bacon grease; fry the onion, fresh garlic, and cauliflower over a medium heat.

When the cauliflower begins to turn brown, add the rest of the seasoning and bacon. Mix well and serve immediately.

Delicious Pepper Flake Sausage and Eggs

Ingredients:

½ pound pork (finely ground)

½ teaspoon of sage (dried)

Salt and pepper as required

A pinch of flaked red pepper (replace with garlic powder if you want something with a little less zing)

¼ sweet onion (diced finely)

¼ cup of zucchini (diced)

12 free range eggs

1 big avocado (cubed)

Directions:

Set your oven to 350°F.

Set your stove at medium heat and warm up a large frying pan. Season the pork and fry until it loses all traces of pink. Remove the pork and set to one side, taking care to leave the grease in the frying pan.

Fry the zucchini and onion until they are tender. (It will take around five minutes). Mix the onion/ zucchini and pork together. Mix in the eggs until well-combined.

Grease a muffin pan with 12 compartments using coconut oil. Divide the mixture between all the compartments.

Bake for about half an hour or until the egg is completely cooked. Serve with some avocado on top.

Spinach Scallions and Egg Bake

Ingredients:

4 cups of freshly picked, young spinach leaves

1 tablespoon of light olive oil

½ cup of mild mozzarella (grated)

½ cup of Colby jack (shredded, or cheddar if you prefer)

¼ cup of scallions (finely chopped)

8 free range eggs

Salt and pepper to taste

Directions:

Set your oven at 375°F. Set your stove at medium heat. Heat the olive oil in a medium to large frying pan.

Add in the spinach and cook quickly until it wilts. Put the spinach in a baking dish. Mix together the rest of the ingredients until completely combined and pour over the spinach.

Bake for around half an hour, so that the eggs are cooked throughout. Serve straight away.

Avocado with Egg and Bacon Stuffing

Ingredients:

2 big avocados

4 rashers of bacon, cooked until crispy and crumbled

4 free range eggs

Salt and pepper to taste

Directions:

Set your oven to 400°F.

Half the avocados and discard the pit. Remove some of the flesh, so that you have a well in the avocado halves. Divide the bacon evenly between the avocado halves. Crack an egg into each of the avocado halves.

Season to taste and put onto a baking tray.

Bake for around 15 minutes or until the egg is cooked to your liking.

Perfect Keto Sausage Casserole

Ingredients:

1 lb. pork sausage

2 cups diced zucchini

2 cups green cabbage, shredded

½ cup diced onion

3 large eggs

½ cup mayonnaise

2 tsp. prepared yellow mustard

1 tsp. dried ground sage

1 ½ cups cheddar cheese, shredded and divided

Cayenne pepper to taste

Directions:

1. Preheat your oven to 375F and grease a casserole dish; set aside.

2. Brown sausage in a large skillet over medium heat until almost cooked through.

3. Add cabbage, zucchini and onion, cooking until vegetables are tender and sausage is fully cooked.

4. Remove from heat and spoon into prepared casserole dish, then set aside.

5. In a mixing bowl, whisk eggs, mayonnaise, mustard, sage, and pepper until smooth.

6. Add 1 cup of the grated cheese to the egg mixture and stir.

7. Pour this mixture over the sausage and vegetables in the casserole dish.

8. Top casserole with the remaining ½ cup cheese.

9. Place casserole in preheated oven and bake 30 minutes, or until bubbling around the edges and the cheese is melted and lightly browned on top.

10. Remove from the oven and serve immediately.

The consistency of this finished dish is on the custard side, with a rich cheddar sauce and just a hint of heat from ground cayenne pepper. If you aren't a fan of the spice, simply omit it but it adds a nice balance to the dish.

Spinach Egg White Omelet

Ingredients

- 5 Egg whites

- 1 Egg yolk

- 2 Tsp Almond milk

- 1 Tomato

- ½ cup Shredded spinach

- Purple onion (1 tbs)

- Basil (1 pinch)

- Garlic (optional)

- Olive oil cooking spray

Directions

- Cut the vegetables

- Beat the egg whites, the yolk and the almond drain.

- Splash a little skillet with oil and snappy sauté the vegetables just until delicate!

- Put the vegetables as an afterthought, splash the skillet once more, put medium-low warmth and pours the eggs. Cook until the eggs are firm, include the vegetables one side and overlay the other half over top.

Serve and enjoy!

Low-Carb Cinnamon Coffee Protein Shake

Ingredients

- 1 scoop Vanilla Iso-Flex Isolate Protein Powder

- 1 shot of espresso

- ¼ cup of greek yogurt

- Pinch of stevia

- Pinch of cinnamon

- 5 ice cubes

Directions:

1. Have your coffee ready

2. Add all the necessary ingredients and the protein powder last in the blender

3. Blend until smooth.

4. ENJOY!

Coconut Savory Sage and Cheddar Waffles

Ingredients:

1 1/3 cup coconut flour, sifted

3 tsp. baking powder

1 tsp. dried ground sage

½ tsp. salt

¼ tsp. garlic powder

2 cups canned coconut milk

½ cup water

2 whole eggs

3 Tbsp. coconut oil, melted

1 cup cheddar cheese, shredded

Directions:

1. Heat your waffle iron according to manufacturer's directions, at a moderate heat.

2. In a mixing bowl whisk together flour, baking powder, and seasonings.

3. Add liquid ingredients, then stir until a stiff batter forms.

4. Mix in the cheese.

5. Liberally grease top and bottom panels of the waffle iron, then place a 1/3-cup scoop of batter onto each iron section. Close the iron and cook until steam rises from the machine and the top panel opens freely without sticking to the waffle. Proper cooking usually takes 2 cycles at moderate heat.

Tip: Time your first batch to make sure you get a precise cooking time, as waffle irons differ and can cause variance in results.

Garlic Spinach Mushroom Quiche

Ingredients

- 4 oz. button mushrooms, sliced
- 5 oz. frozen spinach, thawed
- 1 clove garlic, minced
- ½ cup milk

- 2 large eggs, whisked

- 2 tablespoons parmesan, grated

- 1 oz. feta cheese

- ¼ cup mozzarella grated

- Salt & pepper to taste

Directions:

1. Preheat the oven to 350 F. Press & remove the excess moisture from the spinach.
2. Place a non-stick skillet on medium heat and spray cooking spray over it. Add mushroom and garlic and sauté until gets fully cooked and become soft.
3. Grease a pie dish with cooking spray. Spread the spinach on the pie dish and layer it with sautéed mushrooms. Top it up with crumbled feta cheese.
4. Mix together Parmesan, milk and whisked eggs. Add pepper and stir.
5. Pour into the pie dish. Sprinkle mozzarella over it.
6. Place a baking sheet in the oven and put the pie dish over it and bake until golden brown.
7. Slice and serve.

Avocado Broccoli Frittata

Ingredients

- 5 eggs, whisked
- 1 tablespoon olive oil
- 1 ounce gouda cheese, crumbled
- 1 small head broccoli, chopped into small florets
- 1 medium tomato, chopped
- 1/2 teaspoon pepper powder
- 1 small avocado, peeled, pitted, sliced

Directions:

1. Add eggs, broccoli, tomato, salt and pepper to a bowl and whisk well.
2. Add cheese and mix until well combined.
3. Place an ovenproof pan over medium heat. Add oil and swirl the pan so that the oil spreads.
4. Add the egg mixture and cook until the sides are slightly set.
5. Remove from heat.
6. Bake in a preheated oven at 425 degrees F for about 20-30 minutes or until golden brown.
7. Slice and serve with avocado slices.

Delicious French toast

Ingredients:

For protein bread:

- 6 eggs separated

- 2 oz. cream cheese

- ½ cup egg white

For French toast:

- 1 egg

- ½ teaspoon vanilla

- ¼ cup coconut milk or almond milk

- ½ teaspoon cinnamon powder.

For syrup:

- ¼ cup butter

- ¼ cup almond milk

- ¼ cup swerve confectioners.

Directions:

1. To make bread: Beat the egg whites until very stiff.

2. Add protein powder into the egg whites and mix gently. Add cream cheese and fold gently.

3. Grease a bread pan and pour the dough into it.

4. Put it in the preheated oven at 325 degrees F and bake it until golden brown.

5. Slice the bread when completely cooled down. Make 9 slices.

6. To make French toast: Put a greased skillet on medium high flame.

7. Mix 1 egg, almond milk, vanilla and cinnamon in a bowl.

8. Coat bread slices with egg whites.

9. Grill bread slices on hot skillets until golden brown. Repeat with remaining slices.

10. To make syrup: Melt butter over high heat in a saucepan. Add swerve and milk immediately. Whisk constantly until smooth. Remove from heat and cool. Store in an airtight container in the refrigerator.

11. Top French toast with syrup and serve.

Basil Egg Muffins Cups

Ingredients:

- 6 Eggs

- 6 slices Nitrate Free Shaved Turkey

- ½ cup Sliced Spinach

- 3 tablespoons Red Pepper

- Mozzarella Cheese Light

- Fresh Basil

- Red Onion (2 table spoons, finely chopped)

- Salt & Pepper

Directions:

- Preheat the oven to 350°;

- Cut the spinach, red onion, red pepper and basil and mesh the mozzarella cheddar.

- Shower a nonstick biscuit tin with olive oil splash;

- Delicately wrap the bit of turkey in one of the biscuit glasses with the goal that it lays on the base and the sides of the tin to make a bigger container.

- Deliberately split an egg and empty it into the turkey glass.

- Include a smidgen of cut red onion, spinach, red pepper and cheddar on top of the egg.

- Include some crisp basil and pound a touch of new pepper and salt onto the egg.

- Add the biscuit tin in the broiler and prepare until eggs are set and the whites are murky, around 10 minutes for a runny yolk and more like 15 minutes for a harder one.

Remember that the egg biscuits will cook for somewhat longer when you remove it from the broiler.

Superior One Skillet Bacon and Eggs

Ingredients:

- 1 tablespoon butter

- 8 slices meaty bacon

- 1 carrot, peeled into thin strips

- ½ cup chopped broccoli or cauliflower

- ½ cup finely chopped celery

- ½ large white onion, chopped into small pieces

- 4 large organic eggs

- ½ cup shredded Colby jack cheese

Directions:

- Slice the bacon over the grain into little strips.

- Over medium warmth, dissolve the margarine in a vast skillet. Include the vegetables and bacon.

- Stirring frequently, saute the bacon and vegetables in the margarine for around 20 minutes, until the bacon begins to fresh on the edges and the vegetables start to caramelize.

- Spread the blend over the skillet equally, and after that make a well in each quarter area.

- Break one egg into each well. Keep cooking until the eggs are practically done. If it's all the same to you cooked yolks, simply put a cover over the skillet and let the eggs steam until cooked through.

- When the eggs are practically done, sprinkle the cheddar over the top and let cook somewhat more until the cheddar dissolves.

Rather than utilizing broccoli, carrots and celery, utilize 6-8 ounces of turnips cut in a little dice, and try to cook the onions and turnips sufficiently long to give them a chance to caramelize a bit. The outcome tastes simply like hash browns!

Serve hot. Enjoy!

Tasty Italian Omelet

Ingredients

- 6 eggs

- 3 ounces full fat Brie cheese, sliced

- 3 tablespoons butter

- 15 Kalamata olives, pitted

- 3 tablespoons MCT oil

- 1/2 teaspoon salt

- 1 1/2 teaspoons Herbes De Provence

- 1 large avocado, peeled, pitted, cut into thick slices

Directions:

1. Add eggs, oil, herbes de Provence, olives and salt. Whisk well.

2. Place a nonstick skillet over medium - high heat. Add butter. When the butter melts, add avocado and fry until golden brown all over. Remove and set aside.

3. Place the skillet back on high heat. Add the egg mixture into it.

4. Place the cheese slice on the egg. Cover and cook until the underside is golden brown.

5. Flip sides and cook the other side too. Remove from the pan.

6. Slice into 6 wedges. Top with avocado slices and serve.

Mini Pumpkin Spice Muffins

Ingredients:

3/4 cup canned pumpkin

1/4 cup organic no sugar added sunflower seed butter

1 large egg, room temperature

1/2 cup erythritol

1/4 cup organic coconut flour, sifted

2 Tbsp. organic flaxseed meal

1 tsp. ground cinnamon

1/2 tsp. ground nutmeg

1/2 tsp. baking soda

1/2 tsp. baking powder

1/4 tsp. salt

Optional topping: ½ tsp. plain cream cheese per muffin (you will need 3 Tbsp. of cream cheese for all the muffins.)

Directions:

1. Preheat your oven to 350F then lightly grease a mini muffin pan. You will need 18 sections to bake this entire recipe. Then in a mixing bowl combine pumpkin, sunflower seed butter, and the egg. Stir until smooth.

2. Add all of remaining dry ingredients.

3. Stir to blend.

4. Using a 1-tablespoon measuring spoon, scoop batter into the prepared pan. Bake 15 minutes, then remove the pan from the oven and allow to cool completely.

5. Carefully remove the muffins from the pan and transfer to a serving tray. You can optionally top the muffins with cream cheese.

6. Store in a sealed container at room temperature for up to 3 days. You may also refrigerate these muffins up to 1 week, or freeze up to 1 month. They are best when warmed slightly if refrigerated or frozen. If freezing, do not top with cream cheese until thawed and ready to serve.

Store in a sealed container at room temperature up to 3 days. You may also refrigerate these muffins up to 1 week, or freeze up to 1 month. They are best when warmed slightly if refrigerated or frozen. If freezing, do not top with cream cheese until thawed and ready to serve.

Delicious Broccoli and Cheese Omelet

Ingredients:

- 4 egg whites

- 2 eggs

- 1 cup broccoli, chopped into small pieces, cooked

- 2 tablespoons almond milk

- Salt to taste

- Pepper powder to taste

- 2 slices Swiss cheese

- Cooking spray

Directions:

1. Add eggs, whites, milk, salt and pepper to a bowl and whisk well.

2. Place a nonstick skillet over medium heat. Spray with cooking spray.

3. When the pan is heated, add half the egg mixture. Swirl the pan so that the egg spreads.

4. Place a slice of cheese at the center of the omelet. Place half the broccoli over the cheese.

5. Cook until the egg sets. Fold the sides over the broccoli. Remove on to a plate and serve.

6. Repeat the above 3 steps with the remaining eggs and broccoli.

Basil Cucumber Pancakes

Ingredients

- 3 Cucumbers, shredded

- 3 eggs

- 2 ½ cups almond flour

- 3 tsp. dried parsley

- 2 tsp. dried basil

- Salt and Pepper as per taste

- 3 tbsp. Butter or cooking oil

Method

1. In a medium sized mixing bowl, add the shredded cucumber, the almond flour and the basil.

2. Mix all the ingredients well. When the cucumber is mixed well with the flour, add the pepper and salt and the parsley to the mixture.

3. Make sure that the taste of the mixture is well balanced, so adjust the herbs and seasoning as per your liking.

4. You can make about 12 - 13 patties from the mixture.

5. Heat a large non–stick saucepan on a medium flame.

6. Add one-teaspoon butter or oil to the pan. Once the butter has started warming up, add the patties and cook them on both sides till they are well done.

7. Remove the patty from the pan once they become golden brown on both sides.

Ketogenic Pork Bagel

Ingredients:

- 1 pound ground pork

- 1 onion, finely diced

- 1/3 cup tomato sauce

- 1 tablespoon ghee or butter

- 1 large egg

- Pepper powder to taste

- ½ teaspoon salt or as per taste

- ½ teaspoon paprika

- Lettuce for filling

- Tomato slices for filling

- 1 Avocado

Directions:

1. Heat a skillet over medium heat and add some ghee. Once heated, add the onions and sauté until they get translucent. Remove the onions and keep aside in a bowl.

2. Add the rest of the ingredients to the bowl and mix them well.

3. Once done, divide the mixture into 3 parts and make a ball each of the divided mix. Then make a dent in the middle of the ball, so that it resembles a bagel. Repeat the same procedure with the remaining 2 portions.

4. Keep in a lined baking dish and bake in an oven at 400 degree F for about 35 minutes or until the meat gets cooked.

5. When the bagels cool down, slice them and fill with tomato slices and lettuce and serve.

Mayo Chicken Omelet

Ingredients:

- 2 eggs

- 2 cooked bacon slices

- ¼ of ripe avocado

- 1 ounce cooked chicken pieces

- 1 medium-sized tomato

- 1 tablespoon mayo

- 1 teaspoon mustard paste

Directions:

1. Crack eggs into a medium-sized bowl and beat using whisker.

2. Place a non-stick medium-sized saucepan over medium heat and let heat completely.

3. Add beaten eggs to pan and let cook for 5 minutes or until cooked halfway, then pull the sides of omelet to the center of the pan.

4. Then add bacon, avocado, chicken, tomato, mayo and mustard to one-half of the omelet and then fold in the other half.

5. Cover pan with lid and cook for another 5 minutes or until cook through.

6. Serve warm.

Cheesy Salmon Mug Muffin

Ingredients:

- 0.9-ounce almond flour

- 1.3-ounce flax meal

- ¼ teaspoon baking soda

- 1/8 teaspoon salt

- 2 tablespoons coconut milk, full-fat

- 2 tablespoons water

- 1 egg

- 2.1 ounce smoked salmon, sliced

- 2 tablespoons chopped spring onion

- 2.1-ounce cream cheese, full-fat

Directions:

1. In a medium-sized mixing bowl place almond flour, flax meal, baking soda and salt and stir until just mix.

2. Add milk and water to flour mixture, crack the egg and using a fork stir until mix well.

3. Add sliced salmon and spring onion to the muffin mixture and stir until combine.

4. Divide mixture in an equal portion between two microwave oven proof ramekins and then place in a microwave.

5. Microwave for 60-90 seconds on high heat setting or until done.

6. Remove ramekins carefully from oven, then top with cream cheese and serve straight away.

Protein Mug Muffin

Ingredients:

- 0.9-ounce almond flour

- 1.3-ounce flax meal

- ¼ teaspoon baking soda

- 1/8 teaspoon salt

- 2 tablespoons coconut milk, full-fat

- 1 egg

- 1.1-ounce red pesto

- 1.1-ounce cream cheese, full-fat

- Half of an avocado, sliced

- 2.1-ounce bacon slices, crisped

- 2 tomato slices

Directions:

1. In a medium-sized mixing bowl place almond flour, flax meal, baking soda and salt and stir until just mix.

2. Add milk into flour mixture, crack the egg and using a fork stir until mix well.

3. Add pesto to the muffin mixture and stir until combine.

4. Divide mixture in an equal portion between two microwave oven proof ramekins and then place in a microwave.

5. Microwave for 60-90 seconds on high heat setting or until done.

6. Remove ramekins carefully from oven and set aside until cool completely.

7. Take out cool muffin from each ramekin and then cut in half.

8. Spread cream cheese on both halves of muffin, then top with an avocado slice, bacon and tomato slice, serve straight away.

Turkey Bacon Skillet

Ingredients:

- 3 slices turkey bacon, cut into 1/2 inch pieces

- 3 egg whites

- 1/4 cup red and green bell pepper, chopped

- 1/4 cup onions, chopped

- 1 tablespoon olive oil

- 1/6 teaspoon garlic powder

- 1/4 teaspoon pepper powder or to taste

- 1/4 cup part skim mozzarella cheese, grated

- Salt to taste

Directions:

1. Heat a skillet over medium flame. Add the onion, red and green bell peppers, garlic powder and the turkey bacon.

2. Sauté the ingredients until the bacon gets cooked and brown and the vegetables become slightly soft.

3. Add the egg whites and keep stirring until the eggs are cooked well.

4. Sprinkle cheese on the eggs and season with salt and pepper. Let it cook till the cheese melts.

5. Mix well and serve.

Healthy Porridge

Ingredients:

- 4-ounce hemp hearts

- 2 tablespoons ground flax seeds

- 1 tablespoon chia seeds

- ½ teaspoon ground cinnamon

- 8 fluid ounce coconut milk, full-fat

- 5 drops liquid Stevia

- ¾ teaspoon vanilla extract

- ¼ cup almond flour

- 1 tablespoon pumpkin seeds

Directions:

1. Place a small saucepan over medium heat; add hemp hearts, flax seeds, chia seeds and cinnamon.

2. Pour in milk, then stir in Stevia and vanilla until just combine and bring the mixture to boil.

3. When the mixture starts boiling, stir once and then cook for 2 minutes.

4. After two minutes cooking, remove the pan from heat, stir in almond flour until blend and spoon porridge into a serving bowl.

5. Top with pumpkin seeds and serve immediately.

Garlic Zucchini & Bacon Hash

Ingredients:

- 1 tablespoon coconut oil

- 7-ounce zucchini, diced

- 2.1-ounce bacon slices, chopped

- 1 garlic clove, peeled and chopped

- 1 tablespoon chopped parsley

- ¼ teaspoon salt

- 1 egg, fried

Directions:

1. Place a medium-sized non-stick frying pan over medium-high heat.

2. Grease pan with coconut oil, add garlic and cook for 1 minute or until fragrant.

3. Add bacon and cook for 3 minutes or until nicely light brown, stir occasionally.

4. Add zucchini pieces to the pan and cook for 10 minutes or until done, stir occasionally.

5. When zucchini is cooked through, remove the pan from heat, stir in parsley and transfer to a serving plate.

6. Top with fried egg and serve immediately.

Yummy Beef Breakfast Burger

Ingredients:

- 1 tablespoon coconut oil, melted

- 6-ounce ground beef

- ½ teaspoon salt

- ½ teaspoon ground black pepper

- 1 egg

- 2 bacon slices

- 1 lettuce leaf

- 1 tomato slice

Directions:

1. In a bowl place ground beef, add salt and pepper, stir until mix well and then shape into a burger patty.

2. Place a medium sized non-stick frying pan over medium heat, add oil and heat until hot.

3. Add burger patty into the pan and cook for 3-4 minutes per side or until cook through.

4. Remove cooked patty from the pan and reserve the pan.

5. Crack the egg into the pan, sprinkle with a pinch of pepper and fry.

6. Begin assembling burger by placing a burger patty on half of the lettuce leaf, top with bacon slices, fried egg and tomato slice and wrap with the other half of the lettuce leaf.

7. Serve immediately.

Cheesy Breakfast Tacos

Ingredients:

- 4 keto tacos

- ½ pound pork sausage, cooked

- Half of avocado, peeled and pitted

- 1 egg

- ¼ teaspoon salt

- ¼ teaspoon ground black pepper

- 4 tablespoons sour cream

- 2 tablespoons shredded cheddar cheese

- ½ cup chopped cilantro

Directions:

1. Place a griddle pan over heat and heat until hot.

2. When hot, crack an egg, break the yolk, season with salt and black pepper and cook for 1 minute per side.

3. In the meantime, place a medium-sized pan over medium heat and let heat.

4. Add pork sausage and heat for 3-5 minutes or until warm.

5. Transfer cooked egg from griddle pan and then heat tortillas for 2 minutes per side until warm.

6. Slice avocado

7. Begin assembling tacos by slicing egg into four strips and then layer each tortilla with an egg strip.

8. Top with sausage, then a slice of avocado, followed by spooning sour cream.

9. Sprinkle with cheese and cilantro and serve immediately.

Chapter 3 KETOGENIC LUNCH

Italian Chicken Marinade

Ingredients

1 (16 ounce) bottle Italian-style salad dressing

1 teaspoon garlic powder

1 teaspoon salt

4 skinless, boneless chicken breast halves

Directions

In a shallow baking dish, mix the salad dressing, garlic powder, and salt. Place the chicken in the bowl, and turn to coat. Marinate in the refrigerator at least 4 hours. (For best results, marinate overnight.)

Preheat the grill for high heat.

Lightly oil grate. Discard marinade, and grill chicken 8 minutes on each side, or until juices run clear.

Garlic Roast Chicken

Ingredients

1/2 cup dry white wine

2 lemons, cut in half

6 large cloves garlic

1 (4 pound) whole chicken

1 1/2 teaspoons cold butter

2 tablespoons Dijon mustard

Salt and pepper to taste

Directions

Preheat an oven to 425 degrees F (220 degrees C). Pour the wine into a 10-inch cast-iron skillet; set aside.

Place the lemon halves and garlic cloves into the cavity of the chicken. Slide half of the butter underneath the skin of each breast. Rub the chicken all over with Dijon mustard, then season to taste with salt and pepper. Place into the cast-iron skillet.

Bake the chicken in the preheated oven for 15 minutes, then reduce heat to 350 degrees F (175 degrees C), and continue baking until no longer pink at the bone and the juices run clear, about 1 hour more. An instant-read thermometer inserted into the thickest part of the thigh, near the bone should read 180 degrees F (82 degrees C).

Remove the chicken from the oven, cover with a doubled sheet of aluminum foil, and allow to rest in a warm area for 15 minutes before slicing.

Butter Garlic Baked Chicken

Ingredients

1/2 cup crushed dry-roasted, salted peanuts

1/2 teaspoon garlic powder

1/2 teaspoon onion powder

1 teaspoon salt-free herb seasoning blend

6 chicken thighs, skinned

1/2 cup melted butter

Directions

Preheat oven to 375 degrees F (190 degrees C).

In a shallow bowl, mix the peanuts, garlic powder, onion powder, and salt-free herb seasoning blend.

Dip the chicken thighs in the melted butter, then press into the peanuts to coat. Arrange on a baking sheet.

Bake 45 minutes in the preheated oven, or until chicken juices run clear.

Broiled Mayonnaise Ginger Chicken

Ingredients

4 pounds skinless, boneless chicken breast halves

1/2 cup mayonnaise

1 tablespoon soy sauce

1/4 teaspoon ground ginger

1/8 teaspoon cayenne pepper

Directions

Flatten the chicken to 1/4-in. thickness. Place on a broiler pan rack. Broil for 3 minutes on each side.

Combine mayonnaise, soy sauce, ginger and cayenne; brush over chicken. Broil 2-3 minutes longer on each side or until juices run clear.

Best Kentucky Grilled Chicken

Ingredients

1 cup cider vinegar

1/2 cup vegetable or canola oil

5 teaspoons Worcestershire sauce

4 teaspoons hot pepper sauce

2 teaspoons salt

10 bone-in chicken breast halves

Directions

In a bowl, combine the first five ingredients; mix well. Pour 1 cup marinade into a large resealable plastic bag; add the chicken.

Seal bag and turn to coat; refrigerate for at least 4 hours. Cover and refrigerate the remaining marinade for basting.

Coat grill rack with nonstick cooking spray before starting the grill. Drain and discard marinade from chicken.

Grill bone side down, covered, over indirect medium heat for 20 minutes. Turn; grill 20-30 minutes longer or until juices run clear, basting occasionally with reserved marinade.

Delicious Mushroom Chicken

Ingredients

4 cups sliced fresh mushrooms

3 tablespoons butter, divided

6 (4 ounce) skinless, boneless chicken breast halves

1/4 teaspoon salt

1/4 teaspoon pepper

1/2 cup chicken broth

1/4 cup sherry

Directions

In a large skillet, saute mushrooms in 2 tablespoons butter until tender. Place chicken in a greased shallow 3-qt. baking dish; sprinkle with salt and pepper.

Melt remaining butter; drizzle over chicken. Combine broth and sherry; pour over chicken. Spoon mushrooms over top. Cover and bake at 400 degrees F for 20-25 minutes or until chicken is no longer pink.

Paprika Lemon Stuffed Chicken

Ingredients

1 (3 pound) whole chicken

2 cups stuffing mix

2 lemons

1/4 teaspoon salt

1/4 teaspoon paprika

1/4 teaspoon dried rosemary

1/4 teaspoon dried sage

2 tablespoons olive oil

Directions

Preheat oven to 350 degrees F (175 degrees C).

Stuff the bird with the prepared stuffing and rub the skin with the olive oil. Cut 1 lemon in half; cover the opening of the bird with a lemon half and stuffing (save the other half for garnish).

Pour the juice of the second lemon over the bird. Season the bird with the salt, paprika, rosemary and sage.

Cover and bake in preheated oven for 1 to 2 hours. Remove the cover half way through baking to brown. Baste often.

Garlic Rosemary Pork Roast

Ingredients

3 pounds pork tenderloin

1 tablespoon olive oil

2 cloves garlic, minced

3 tablespoons dried rosemary

Directions

Preheat oven to 375 degrees F (190 degrees C).

Rub the roast OR tenderloin liberally with olive oil, then spread the garlic over it. Place it in a 10x15 inch roasting pan and sprinkle with the rosemary.

Bake at 375 degrees F (190 degrees C) for 2 hours, or until the internal temperature of the pork reaches 160 degrees F (70 degrees C).

Tasty Cumin Spicy Pork Sausage

Ingredients

1 pound fresh, ground pork sausage

1 tablespoon crushed red pepper

1 1/2 tablespoons ground cumin

3 cloves garlic, finely chopped

Salt to taste

Directions

In a bowl, mix together with your hands Pork sausage, red pepper, cumin, garlic and salt. Form patties. Fry in a skillet over medium heat until well done.

Pork Chops Bacon Wrapped

Ingredients

6 (1 inch thick) boneless pork chops

6 tablespoons process cheese sauce

12 slices bacon

Directions

Preheat the oven to 350 degrees F (175 degrees C). Fry the bacon in a skillet over medium heat until cooked through but still flexible. Wrap two slices of bacon around each pork chop and top with a tablespoon of cheese sauce. Place the pork chops in a baking dish.

Bake for 1 hour in the preheated oven.

Onion Mushrooms Pork

Ingredients

4 pork chops

1 (10.75 ounce) can condensed cream of mushroom soup

1 onion, chopped

2/3 cup water

Directions

Preheat oven to 350 degrees F (175 degrees C).

Place pork chops in a 9x13 inch baking dish. In a medium bowl combine the soup, onion and water.

Mix well and pour mixture over pork chops. Cover dish with aluminum foil and bake in the preheated oven for 45 minutes.

Remove cover and bake for another 15 minutes.

Garlic Pork Roast

Ingredients

1 tablespoon vegetable oil

1 (2 pound) boneless pork roast

Salt and pepper to taste

4 sweet potatoes, quartered

1 onion, quartered

6 cloves garlic

1 (14.5 ounce) can chicken broth

Directions

Heat oil in large heavy skillet. Season meat with salt and pepper, and brown in oil.

In a slow cooker, layer sweet potatoes, onion and garlic. Place browned roast on top of vegetables, and pour in chicken broth.

Cover, and cook on low setting for 6 hours.

Yummy Slow Cooker Pork

Ingredients

3 pounds pork shoulder

2 (1 ounce) packages taco seasoning mix

Chili powder to taste

Crushed red pepper to taste

Directions

Place pork shoulder in a slow cooker with taco seasoning. If desired, add chili powder and/or red pepper flakes. Add water until meat is covered. Place lid on pot and cook on low for 8 hours.

Remove pork shoulder from pot and shred.

Garlic Pork with White Wine

Ingredients

2 cloves crushed garlic

1 1/4 pounds boneless loin pork roast

Salt and pepper to taste

1 tablespoon olive oil

1 1/4 cups white wine

1 1/4 cups chicken stock

Directions

Chop up the garlic and rub it into the pork; rub in some salt to taste. Heat oil in a large skillet and brown the pork. Add the pepper to taste, wine and stock and bring all to a boil.

Reduce heat to low, cover skillet and let simmer for 50 to 55 minutes or until internal temperature of pork has reached 160 degrees F (70 degrees C). Cut pork into bite size pieces and serve it in the cooking liquids.

Stir-fry Beef and Broccoli

Ingredients:

- 4 cups broccoli, chopped (florets)

- 1 lb. boneless round steak
- 3 garlic clove, minced
- 1 small onion
- 1 red bell pepper
- ½ cup water
- 2 tablespoons coconut oil
- 1 teaspoon ground ginger
- ½ tablespoon coconut aminos
- Salt and black pepper to taste
- 1 ½ lb. Brussels sprouts
- Cooking fat

Directions:

1. Use a cast-iron skillet cooked over low-medium heat.
2. Add 2 garlic clove, minced, and cook until its golden.
3. Add Brussels sprouts.
4. Add salt and pepper to taste for about 10-15 minutes. After which, set aside.
5. Use the cast-iron skillet cooked over medium heat to stir-fry the beef for about 6-7 minutes. After which, set the beef aside.
6. Now, time to cook the red bell peppers, broccoli and onions together for about 6 minutes.
7. Add your beef back into the mix.
8. Separately, mix water, ground ginger, remaining garlic, coconut aminos, and salt and pepper to taste. After mixing them together, add it to the beef mix for about 3 minutes.
9. Heat up your Brussels sprouts just right.

10. Once done, add your Brussels sprouts and stir-fry beef together. Voila!

Low-Carb Tuna Mayonnaise Meatballs

Ingredients:

280 grams canned tuna fish, drained

1 medium avocado, peeled, pitted and diced

1 cup chopped celery

¼ cup cottage cheese

¼ cup mayonnaise

¼ teaspoon onion powder

¼ teaspoon paprika

1/3 cup almond flour

1 cup olive oil

Pinch of salt and ground black pepper

Directions:

Transfer the tuna to a mixing bowl and season it with salt, onion powder, paprika and pepper. Mix well.

Add in the avocado, celery, cheese and mayonnaise. Slightly mash the ingredients together. Form 12 meatballs from the tuna avocado mixture then roll it in the almond flour. Set aside.

Heat the olive oil in a pan over medium-high flame. Once the oil is hot, fry the meatballs until the sides are golden brown. Let it cool for 5 minutes then serve.

This recipe yields 12 meatballs

Cumin Hot and Spicy Pork Taco Wraps

Ingredients:

10 iceberg or Boston lettuce leaves, washed and drained

400 grams lean ground pork

1 cup tomato salsa

½ teaspoon garlic powder

¼ teaspoon cumin

½ teaspoon onion powder

¼ teaspoon ground black pepper

1 tablespoon olive oil

Slices of avocado, bell peppers and red onions

Directions:

Place the ground pork, garlic powder, cumin, onion powder and black pepper in a bowl. Using your hands, knead the spices into the meat.

Heat the olive oil in a skillet over medium flame. Place the spiced ground pork on the skillet and cook it until the meat becomes brown.

Once the meat is cooked, turn off the flame and drain the excess oil from the cooked pork. Pour the salsa over the pork and mix well.

To assemble the taco wraps, place a lettuce leaf on a plate, spoon the pork mixture on top of it then place some chopped avocadoes, peppers and onions. Fold or roll the lettuce leaf to secure the pork inside it. Serve immediately.

This recipe yields 2 servings.

Pineapple Bacon Meatball Skewers

Ingredients:

5 bacon slices

450 grams ground pork

½ teaspoon salt

½ teaspoon ground black pepper

½ teaspoon onion powder

½ teaspoon garlic powder

½ teaspoon turmeric powder

½ cup olive oil

Chunks of tomato, cucumber and pineapple

Directions:

Place the bacon and ground pork in a food processor and blend well. Season the meatball mixture with salt, pepper, onion powder, garlic powder and turmeric powder.

Form the mixture into 20 meatballs and place it on a parchment-lined baking sheet. Bake the meatballs in a 170°F oven for 12 minutes. Let the meatballs cool on a wire rack for 10 minutes.

To serve, place a chunk of tomato, cucumber, pineapple and meatball through a small skewer. Place the skewers on a serving plate and drizzle with olive oil.

This recipe yields 10 servings.

Zesty Chili Crab Cakes

Ingredients:

3 cups fresh crab meat

2 large eggs

2 tablespoon coconut flour

4 tablespoons minced green chilies

1 tablespoon minced garlic

1 teaspoon Dijon mustard

½ teaspoon mayonnaise

Pinch of sea salt and black pepper

3 tablespoons olive oil

Directions:

In a large bowl, mix together the crab meat, eggs, chilies, garlic, mustard and mayonnaise. Season the mixture with salt and pepper then gradually add the coconut flour to thicken its consistency. Mix well.

Form the mixture into 10 round patties and set aside.

Heat the olive oil in a large pan over medium-high flame. Place the crab cakes on the pan and cook each side for 3 minutes or until golden brown.

This recipe yields 10 servings.

Ginger Spicy Pork Tenderloin

Ingredients

2 tablespoons chili powder

1 teaspoon salt

1/4 teaspoon ground ginger

1/4 teaspoon dried thyme

1/4 teaspoon ground black pepper

2 (1 pound) pork tenderloins

Directions

In a small bowl, mix together chili powder, salt, ginger, thyme, and black pepper. Rub spice mix into pork tenderloins. Place meat in a baking dish, cover, and refrigerator for 2 to 3 hours.

Preheat grill for medium heat.

Brush oil onto grill grate, and arrange meat on grill. Cook for 30 minutes, or to desired doneness, turning to cook evenly.

Delicious Steamed Corned Beef

Ingredients

1 (12 ounce) can corned beef

1/4 green bell pepper, chopped

1/4 onion, chopped

1 teaspoon vegetable oil

2 teaspoons tomato paste

1/4 cup water

1/4 teaspoon crushed red pepper flakes

1/4 teaspoon dried thyme

Salt and pepper to taste

Directions

Heat the oil in a skillet over medium heat. Add onion, green pepper, red pepper flakes and dried thyme; cook and stir until the onion is beginning to brown, about 7 minutes.

Reduce the heat to low and stir in the tomato paste and season with salt and pepper.

Simmer for 3 minutes then stir in the water.

Mix in the corned beef and then let it simmer until most of the liquid has evaporated

Onion Oven-Dried Beef Jerky

Ingredients

1 1/2 pounds beef round steak

1/4 cup soy sauce

1 tablespoon Worcestershire sauce

1/2 teaspoon onion salt

1/4 teaspoon garlic powder

1/4 teaspoon pepper

Directions

Trim and discard all fat from meat. Cut meat into 5-in. x 1/2-in. strips. In a large resealable plastic bag, combine the remaining ingredients; add meat. Seal bag and toss to coat.

Refrigerate for 8 hours or overnight.

Place wire racks on foil-lined baking sheets. Drain and discard marinade. Place meat strips 1/4 in. apart on racks.

Bake, uncovered, at 200 degrees F for 6-7 hours or until meat is dry and leathery. Remove from the oven; cool completely. Refrigerate or freeze in an airtight container.

Green Beans Pork

Ingredients:

- 1 pork tenderloin (4 oz)

- 1 cup steamed green beans

- 2 Tbsp sliced almonds

- 1 baked sweet potato

Directions:

Season pork with salt and pepper, singe in an ovenproof skillet covered with cooking shower, and exchange to a 450°F stove for 15 minutes, cut and present with green beans finished with almonds, and a sweet potato.

Healthy Black Beans Pizza

Ingredients:

- 1 Amy's Light 'N Lean Italian Vegetable Pizza

- 3 oz broccoli slaw

- 1/4 cup black beans

- 1/4 cup sliced scallions

- 1 tsp olive oil

- 1 oz lemon juice

Directions:

Bake pizza. Blend together slaw, beans, scallions, oil, and lemon juice, and serve on the side.

Mushrooms Chicken and Sweet Potato

Ingredients:

- 1/2 skinless chicken breast

- 1 cup baby portobello mushrooms, sliced

- 1 Tbsp chives

- 1 Tbsp olive oil

- 1 medium sweet potato

Directions:

In a 350°F stove, prepare chicken, finished with mushrooms, chives, and oil, for 15 minutes. Microwave sweet potato for five to seven minutes.

Lemon Shrimp Ceviche

Ingredients:

- 1/2 cup chopped cucumber

- 1/3 cup chopped jicama

- 1/3 cup chopped mango

- 1 Tbsp chopped onion

- 1/4 cup sliced avocado

- 1 tomato, sliced

- 1 cup cooked shrimp

- 1/4 cup lemon juice

- 1 tsp red pepper

Directions:

Toss all together, and dress with lemon juice.

Chilli Yummy Lasagna

Ingredients:

- 1/2 cup cooked whole-wheat spaghetti

- 1/4 cup part-skim ricotta

- 1/3 cup prepared tomato sauce

- 1/2 tsp crushed red chili flakes

- 1 Coleman Natural Mild Italian Chicken Sausage link, cooked

- 2 cups spinach

Directions:

Combine pasta, ricotta, sauce, and chili flakes, and then crumble sausage on top. Also include spinach, and let wilt.

Cheesy Broccoli Chicken Soup

Ingredients:

- 1 cup chopped broccoli

- 1 cup chopped parsnips

- 3/4 cup nonfat chicken stock

- 1/4 cup low-fat shredded cheddar cheese

- 1 Tbsp sliced almonds

- 4 oz chicken breast

- 1 tsp lemon juice

- Salt and pepper, to taste

Directions:

Steam broccoli & parsnips, and then puree with stock & cheddar; also sprinkle with nuts.

Bake chicken, top with lemon juice, as well as season.

Wild Rice Cilantro Shrimp with Squash

Ingredients:

- 8 large shrimp

- 1 Tbsp olive oil

- 2 tsp fresh cilantro

- · 2 tsp fresh lime juice

- · 1 yellow squash, sliced

- · 1 cup Swiss chard

- · 1/4 cup dry wild rice blend

Directions:

Singe shrimp in olive oil over medium warmth for three to four minutes, flavoring with cilantro and lime juice.

Steam squash and chard for five to seven minutes, and cook rice as per package directions.

Garlic Sesame Beef Bites

Ingredients

2 tablespoons sesame oil

1 tablespoon rice vinegar

1 green onion, minced

1 clove garlic, minced

2 teaspoons hoisin sauce

1/4 teaspoon chili garlic sauce

1 pound beef tenderloin, cut into 3/4 inch cubes

1/4 cup teriyaki sauce

1/2 teaspoon sesame seeds

Directions

Whisk together the sesame oil, vinegar, green onion, garlic, hoisin sauce, and chili garlic sauce in a large glass or ceramic bowl. Add the beef tenderloin cubes and toss to evenly coat.

Cover the bowl with plastic wrap and marinate at room temperature for 10 minutes, or in the refrigerator up to 8 hours.

Preheat the oven's broiler and set the oven rack about 6 inches from the heat source. Line a baking sheet with aluminum foil.

Spread the beef cubes onto the prepared baking sheet. Bake in the preheated oven until cooked to your desired degree of doneness, about 8 minutes for medium-well.

Transfer to a bowl and toss with teriyaki sauce. Skewer each piece of beef with a toothpick and place onto a serving platter. Sprinkle with sesame seeds to serve.

Soy Sauce Beef Kelaguen

Ingredients

1 1/2 cups lemon juice

2 tablespoons soy sauce

Tabasco to taste

1 bunch green onions, thinly sliced

2 pounds beef flank steak, very thinly sliced against the grain

Directions

Pour lemon juice, soy sauce, and Tabasco in a large, glass bowl. Stir in the green onions and beef. Add additional lemon juice if needed to cover the beef.

Cover the bowl with plastic wrap, and allow to rest at room temperature for one hour, until the meat turns a grayish-brown color and appears cooked.

Garlic American Roast Beef

Ingredients

3 pounds beef eye of round roast

1/2 teaspoon kosher salt

1/2 teaspoon garlic powder

1/4 teaspoon freshly ground black pepper

Directions

Preheat oven to 375 degrees F (190 degrees C). If roast is untied, tie at 3 inch intervals with cotton twine.

Place roast in pan, and season with salt, garlic powder, and pepper. Add more or less seasonings to taste.

Roast in oven for 60 minutes (20 minutes per pound). Remove from oven, cover loosely with foil, and let rest for 15 to 20 minutes.

Onion Beef Bacon Rolls

Ingredients

1 1/2 pounds top sirloin, lean

1 pound bacon

1 cup chopped onion

1 1/3 cups butter

Directions

Cut the beef into strips that are approximately 1 inch wide and the same length or close to the length of the bacon strip, about 1/8 inch thick. Serve hot.

Make the beef bacon rolls by laying a strip of bacon on a strip of beef and rolling the two meats together so that the beef is on the outside when you finish rolling. Insert a toothpick so that it goes in on the bottom left side and comes out the top right side when looked at vertically.

In large skillet, saute onions and butter until onions are tender. Lay a single layer of beef bacon rolls in the skillet. Brown them on medium heat, turning once or twice. Cover the skillet and simmer about 2 hours.

Yummy Skillet Lamb Chops

Ingredients

2 (8 ounce) lamb shoulder blade chops

2 tablespoons vegetable oil

1/2 cup warm water

1 teaspoon lemon juice

1 teaspoon dried minced onion

1/2 teaspoon dried oregano

1/4 teaspoon salt

1/8 teaspoon pepper

Directions

In a large skillet, brown lamb chops in oil. Add the remaining ingredients; bring to a boil. Reduce heat; cover and simmer for 30 -35 minutes or until meat juices run clear.

Red Wine Braised Lamb Shanks

Ingredients

2 large white onions, chopped

4 lamb shanks

2 cups dry red wine

1 cup balsamic vinegar

1/3 cup olive oil

4 cloves garlic, pressed

2 lemons, quartered

2 (14.5 ounce) cans diced tomatoes

1 bunch fresh basil, chopped

1 tablespoon kosher salt

1 tablespoon cracked black pepper

Directions

Preheat the oven to 350 degrees F (175 degrees C).

Place the onions in a layer in the bottom of a Dutch oven or medium roasting pan with a lid. Arrange the lamb shanks on top of the onions. Pour the wine, balsamic vinegar and olive oil over the lamb. Place a clove of pressed garlic next to each shank, and a quarter of a lemon on each side. Pour the tomatoes over everything, then season with salt, pepper and basil.

Cover and place in the preheated oven. Cook for 3 hours. Use juices from the pan to make a nice flavorful gravy.

Olive Oil Thyme Lamb Chops

Ingredients

1/2 cup olive oil

1/4 cup lemon juice

1 tablespoon chopped fresh thyme

Salt and pepper to taste

12 lamb chops

Directions

Stir together olive oil, lemon juice, and thyme in a small bowl. Season with salt and pepper to taste. Place lamb chops in a shallow dish, and brush with the olive oil mixture. Marinate in the refrigerator for 1 hour.

Preheat grill for high heat.

Lightly oil grill grate. Place lamb chops on grill, and discard marinade. Cook for 10 minutes, turning once, or to desired doneness.

Delicious Lamb Chops in Duck Sauce

Ingredients

3 pounds lamb chops

2 tablespoons Worcestershire sauce

1 tablespoon adobo seasoning cayenne pepper to taste

Salt and pepper to taste

1 1/2 cups duck sauce

Directions

Preheat oven to 350 degrees F (175 degrees C).

Arrange lamb chops in a medium baking dish, and evenly coat with Worcestershire sauce, adobo seasoning, and cayenne pepper. Season with salt and pepper.

Bake 1 hour in the preheated oven.

Cover lamb chops with duck sauce, and continue baking 15 to 20 minutes, to an internal temperature of 145 degrees F (65 degrees C).

Tasty Roast Leg of Lamb

Ingredients

6 pounds leg of lamb

2 garlic cloves, minced

1/2 teaspoon dried thyme

1/2 teaspoon dried marjoram

1/2 teaspoon dried oregano

1/4 teaspoon salt

1/8 teaspoon pepper

1 teaspoon vegetable oil

Directions

Place roast on a rack in a shallow roasting pan. Cut 12-14 slits 1/2 in. deep in roast. Combine garlic, thyme, marjoram, oregano, salt and pepper; spoon 2 teaspoons into the slits. Brush roast with oil; rub with remaining herb mixture.

Bake, uncovered, at 325 degrees F for 2-3 hours or until meat reaches desired doneness (for medium-rare, a meat thermometer should read 145 degrees F; medium, 160 degrees F; well-done 170 degrees F;).

Let stand 10-15 minutes before slicing.

Cumin Garlic Spicy Lamb Patties

Ingredients

1 pound ground lamb

3 green onions, minced

4 cloves garlic, minced

1 tablespoon curry powder

1 teaspoon ground cumin

1/4 teaspoon dried red pepper flakes

Salt and pepper to taste

Directions

Preheat the grill for high heat.

In a bowl, mix the lamb, green onions, garlic, curry powder, cumin, red pepper, salt and pepper. Form into 4 patties.

Lightly oil grill grate. Grill patties 5 minutes on each side, or until done.

Zested Fish in Foil

Ingredients

2 rainbow trout fillets

1 tablespoon olive oil

2 teaspoons garlic salt

1 teaspoon ground black pepper

1 fresh jalapeno pepper, sliced

1 lemon, sliced

Directions

Preheat oven to 400 degrees F (200 degrees C). Rinse fish, and pat dry.

Rub fillets with olive oil, and season with garlic salt and black pepper. Place each fillet on a large sheet of aluminum foil. Top with jalapeno slices, and squeeze the juice from the ends of the lemons over the fish. Arrange lemon slices on top of fillets. Carefully seal all edges of the foil to form enclosed packets. Place packets on baking sheet.

Bake in preheated oven for 15 to 20 minutes, depending on the size of fish. Fish is done when it flakes easily with a fork.

Garlic Fish Fillets Italiano

Ingredients

2 tablespoons olive oil

1 onion, thinly sliced

2 cloves garlic, minced

1 (14.5 ounce) can diced tomatoes

1/2 cup black olives, pitted and sliced

1 tablespoon chopped fresh parsley

1/2 cup dry white wine

1 pound cod fillets

Directions

In a large frying pan, heat oil over medium heat. Saute onions and garlic in olive oil until softened.

Stir in tomatoes, olives, parsley, and wine. Simmer for 5 minutes.

Place fillets in sauce. Simmer for about 5 more minutes, or until fish turns white.

Soy Sauce Five Spices Fish

Ingredients

4 fresh or frozen orange roughy fillets (6 ounces each), thawed

1 tablespoon canola oil

1 cup water

1/3 cup sliced green onions

2 teaspoons cider vinegar

2 teaspoons soy sauce

2 garlic cloves, minced

1/2 teaspoon Chinese five-spice powder

1/8 teaspoon crushed red pepper flakes

1/4 teaspoon salt

1/4 teaspoon ground ginger

1/2 teaspoon sesame oil

Directions

In a large nonstick skillet, cook fish in canola oil for 2 minutes. Turn and cook 2 minutes longer.

Add the next nine ingredients. Cover and simmer for 4 minutes or until fish flakes easily with a fork. Sprinkle with sesame oil.

Mustard Seafood Dressing

Ingredients

1 cup canned shrimp

2 hard-cooked eggs, chopped

1 1/2 cups finely grated carrots

1 tablespoon minced onion

1/2 teaspoon salt

1/8 teaspoon ground black pepper

1/2 cup mayonnaise

2 tablespoons lemon juice

1/2 teaspoon prepared mustard

4 medium tomatoes

4 leaves of lettuce

Directions

Add shrimp, eggs, carrots, onion, salt, and pepper to the bowl of a food processor. Pulse until just combined.

Blend mayonnaise with lemon juice and mustard; mix into shrimp mixture with a fork.

Core tomatoes. Cut into quarters without cutting all the way to the bottom. Place each tomato on a lettuce leaf, and open.

Spoon shrimp mixture into the center. Serve

Mayonnaise Seafood Stuffed Avocados

Ingredients:

1/2 cup flaked cooked crabmeat

1/2 cup cooked small shrimp

2 tablespoons peeled and diced cucumber

1 tablespoon mayonnaise

1 teaspoon chopped fresh parsley

1 pinch salt

1 pinch ground black pepper

1 pinch paprika

1 avocado

Directions

In a bowl, mix the crab, shrimp, cucumber, mayonnaise, and parsley. Season with salt, and pepper. Cover, and chill until serving.

Slice the avocados lengthwise, and remove the pit. Scoop out the flesh of the avocado, leaving about 1/2 inch on the peel.

Spoon the seafood mixture into the hollowed centers of the avocado halves. Sprinkle the tops with paprika.

Paprika Mustard Seafood Melange

Ingredients

4 sole, patted dry

10 bay scallops, raw

3/4 cup crabmeat

3/4 cup cooked shrimp

1/2 cup shredded Monterey Jack cheese

1/2 cup butter 2 egg yolks

1 tablespoon lemon juice

1/2 teaspoon mustard powder

1/8 teaspoon salt

2 tablespoons chopped fresh parsley

1/4 teaspoon paprika

Directions

Butter two 2-cup au gratin dishes. Place 1 fillet on bottom of each, then layer with scallops, crabmeat, shrimp, cheese and a second fillet; set aside.

Preheat oven to 450 degrees F (230 degrees C).

Melt butter. In a medium mixing bowl, combine yolks, lemon juice, mustard and salt; mix on high and slowly add butter in a steady stream until sauce is thick and creamy. Pour sauce over fillets.

Bake in preheated oven for 10 to 15 minutes; sprinkle with parsley and paprika. Serve.

Yummy Spicy Ground Beef Stew

Ingredients

1 pound ground beef

2 (10.75 ounce) cans condensed vegetable beef soup

1 (10 ounce) can diced tomatoes and green chilies, undrained

Directions

In a large saucepan, cook the beef over medium heat until no longer pink; drain. Stir in soup and tomatoes; heat through.

Oriental Beef Flank

Ingredients

3/4 pound beef flank steak

2 tablespoons teriyaki sauce

1 1/2 teaspoons vegetable oil

1 garlic clove, minced

1/4 teaspoon ground ginger

1/8 teaspoon crushed red pepper flakes

1/2 teaspoon toasted sesame seeds

Directions

Slice meat across the grain into 1/4-in. strips. In a resealable plastic bag, combine the teriyaki sauce, oil, garlic, ginger and red pepper flakes; add meat. Seal bag and turn to coat; refrigerate for 8 hours or overnight, turning several times.

Drain and discard marinade.

Weave meat onto metal or soaked wooden skewers. Grill, covered, over medium heat or broil 4 in. from heat for 2-4 minutes on each side or until desired doneness. Remove from grill or broiler and sprinkle with sesame seeds.

Gravy Mushrooms Pork

Ingredients

2 tablespoons oil

1 pound raw pork shoulder, cut into bite-size cubes

1 large onion, slivered (about 5 ounces)

Seasonings of your choice *

8 ounces fresh mushrooms, sliced

1/4 teaspoon xanthan gum

1/4 cup heavy cream

1 tablespoon dry white wine

Directions

In a large skillet or wok, heat the oil over medium-high heat. Add the pork and onions and the seasonings of your choice.

Cook until the meat is browned on the outside. Cover the pan and turn the heat to low; simmer about 20 minutes until the pork is tender.

Add the mushrooms and cook until tender. Push the pork to one side of the pan so that it's not submerged in the juices.

Sprinkle the xanthan gum over the meat and quickly stir in. Stir until the juices have thickened.

Stir about 1/4 cup of cream and a little wine.

Cook and stir until heated through. If you don't have enough pan juices, you can add a little broth or water to make more gravy.

Makes 4 Servings

Zucchini & Bacon Stir-Fry

Ingredients

4 slices bacon, chopped

1 ounce onion, chopped, 1/4 cup

2 medium zucchini, cut in half moons, 12 ounces

Salt and pepper, to taste

2 eggs, fried in 1 tablespoon butter

Directions

In a medium skillet, fry the bacon until it starts to brown and render its fat. Add the onion and zucchini.

Cook and stir over medium-high heat until the zucchini is tender and caramelized and the bacon is cooked completely.

Season to taste with salt and pepper while cooking. Transfer the zucchini mixture to a serving plate and keep warm.

In the same skillet, fry two eggs in butter. Serve the eggs over the zucchini mixture.

Onion Mushroom Pork Stir-Fry

Ingredients

1 tablespoon oil

2 tablespoons butter

1 pound raw pork shoulder, cut into bite-size strips

1 large onion, slivered (about 5 ounces)

8 ounces fresh mushrooms, sliced

Seasonings of your choice

Directions

In a large skillet or wok, heat the oil and butter over medium-high heat. Add the pork and onions.

Stir-fry until well browned and the pork is done. Add the mushrooms and stir-fry until tender. Season as desired.

Celery Mushroom Ground Beef

Ingredients

2 pounds ground beef

1/3 cup onion, chopped

2 cups celery, chopped

1 clove garlic, minced

1/2 teaspoon salt, or to taste

1/4 teaspoon pepper, or to taste

1 teaspoon beef bouillon granules

1 teaspoon dried dill weed *

1 tablespoon dill pickle relish

8 ounces fresh mushrooms, sliced

8 ounces sour cream

Directions

In a large Dutch oven, brown the ground beef with the onions, celery, garlic, salt and pepper.

Cook until the meat is done and the onions and celery are tender. Drain the grease.

Add all of the remaining ingredients except the sour cream. Simmer about 5 minutes, stirring often, until the mushrooms are cooked.

Remove from the heat and stir in the sour cream.

Adjust the seasonings as needed. Serve over the pasta substitute of your choice, such as zucchini noodles (not included in the counts).

Zucchini Cheesy Beef Casserole

Ingredients

1 1/2 pounds ground beef

2 1/2 ounces onion, chopped fine, 1 small

2 stalks celery, chopped fine

1 clove garlic, minced

1/2 cup tomato sauce

2 teaspoons granular Splenda

1 tablespoon vinegar

1 tablespoon Worcestershire sauce

1 teaspoon mustard

1/2 teaspoon salt

1/4 teaspoon pepper

4 medium zucchini, 28 ounces total

8 ounces cheddar cheese, shredded

Directions

Brown the hamburger, onion, celery and garlic; drain the fat. Add the remaining ingredients.

Simmer, covered, about 10-20 minutes.

Meanwhile, slice the zucchini in half lengthwise, then cut into 1/2" thick, half moons.

Cook until tender, but not too soft; drain well.

Mix the meat mixture, zucchini and cheese in a large casserole; add salt and pepper to taste.

Microwave until hot and bubbly, stirring occasionally.

Cheesy Chicken Broccoli Casserole

Ingredients

2 cups diced cooked chicken

8 ounces frozen broccoli cuts or florets, cooked and drained well

1/4 cup sour cream

1/4 cup mayonnaise

1/2 teaspoon chicken bouillon granules dissolved in 1/4 cup hot water

1 teaspoon garlic powder

4 ounces cheddar cheese, shredded, 1 cup

4 pieces bacon, chopped and fried until crisp

Salt and pepper, to taste

Directions

Put the chicken in a greased 1 1/2 quart casserole; sprinkle with a little salt and pepper.

Top with the broccoli; season with salt and pepper.

In a small bowl, whisk together the sour cream, mayonnaise, bouillon mixture and garlic powder; pour over the broccoli.

Top with cheese the and sprinkle with the bacon.

Bake at 350° 25 minutes until hot and bubbly.

Soy Sauce Marinated Steak Salad

Ingredients

- 2.5 oz. of salad greens

- 6 to 8 pcs. of cherry or grape tomatoes, halved

- ½ pc. of red bell pepper, sliced

- 4 pcs. of radish, sliced

- 1 Tbsp. of olive oil

- ½ Tbsp. of fresh lemon juice

- Salt, to taste

- ½ lb. of steak

- ¼ cup of tamari soy sauce (gluten-free)

- Avocado or olive oil for cooking the steak

Instructions

1. Marinade steak in gluten-free tamari soy sauce.

2. Get a mixing bowl.

3. Start preparing the salad by mixing the tomatoes, bell pepper, salad greens, and radishes with the lemon juice and olive oil. Sprinkle some salt, to taste.

4. Divide and transfer the salad into 2 plates.

5. Put avocado oil (or olive oil) in the frying pan. Set heat on high setting.

6. Cook (or grill) the marinated steak to the preferred doneness level.

7. Transfer the steak into a platter. Set aside for a minute.

8. Slice the steak into strips, and distribute evenly on top of the 2 plates of salad.

Italian Sausage Stir-Fry

Ingredients:

- 2 cups chopped broccoli rabe

- 4 ounces Italian sausage

- 1 tablespoon grated parmesan cheese

- ½ tablespoon olive oil

- 1 garlic clove

- Salt and Pepper as per taste

- 3 cups Water

Directions:

1. Boil salted water in a medium pot. Add the broccoli rabe to the pot and cook it for around two minutes.

2. Drain the excess water once the broccoli turns green.

3. Sauté the sausages in a frying pan.

4. Add the olive oil and the garlic and cook for another two minutes.

5. Toss in the broccoli into the pan and cook for another two minutes.

6. Season it with salt and pepper. Garnish it with the grated Parmesan cheese and serve hot.

Pastrami Rosemary Meaty Stuffed Bell Peppers

Ingredients:

- ½ pound shaved beef steak

- ¼ pound red pastrami, cut into 1 inch pieces

- 1 tablespoon onion, chopped

- 2 green bell peppers, tops removed, deseeded

- A pinch of rosemary

- 1 tablespoon ghee or olive oil

- ½ tablespoon prepared mustard

- 1 ½ tablespoon mayonnaise

- 2 slices cheese

Directions:

1. Heat ghee in a pan on medium flame. Add the onions and sauté until the onions are translucent. Add the steak, rosemary, a pinch of salt and pepper and cook until the steak is browned.

2. Add the pastrami and let it cook. Remove the meat from heat and add the mayonnaise and mustard.

3. Keep the bell peppers on a baking tray in an oven preheated at 350 degrees F and bake for about 2-3 minutes.

4. Remove the bell peppers from the oven and when cool, fill them with the steak mixture. Top with a slice of cheese.

5. Bake the stuffed bell peppers for about 2-3 minutes until the cheese is melted.

6. Serve hot.

Garlic Chicken Bacon Wrapped

Ingredients

- 1 large-sized chicken breast, cut into around 25 bite-sized pieces
- 8 to 9 thin bacon slices, cut into 3 pcs. each
- 6 pcs. of crushed garlic or 3 Tbsp. of garlic powder

Instructions

1. Pre-heat oven to 400° F.

2. Get a baking tray and line with aluminium foil.

3. Put crushed garlic or garlic powder in a mixing bowl

4. Dip each bite-sized chicken piece in garlic.

5. Wrap each piece of chicken with a short piece of bacon.

6. Arrange the bacon-wrapped chicken on the tray. Make sure to have enough space between each chicken piece on the baking tray so they will not touch one another.

7. Place the tray in the oven and bake for 25 to 30 minutes. If possible, turn the chicken pieces after 15 minutes.

Olive Oil Sardines Mustard Salad

Ingredients

- 4 to 5 oz. (1 can) of sardines in olive oil

- ¼ pc. of cucumber, peeled and cut into small dice

- 1 Tbsp. of lemon juice

- ½ Tbsp. of mustard

- Salt & pepper, to taste

Instructions

1. Drain the sardines of excess olive oil.

2. Mash the sardines.

3. Mix the sardines, lemon juice, diced cucumber, mustard and salt & pepper. Make sure the ingredients are well-combined.

4. Transfer the ingredients to a serving dish and serve.

Delicious Chicken Noodle Soup

Ingredients

- 3 cups of chicken broth
- 1 pc. of chicken breast (around ½ lb.), cut into small pcs.
- 1 pc. of green onion, sliced or chopped
- 1 stalk of celery, sliced or chopped
- 1 pc. of zucchini, peeled
- ¼ cup of cilantro, chopped finely
- Salt, to taste

Directions:

1. Dice the chicken breast.
2. Heat a saucepan with avocado oil.
3. Sauté the chicken pieces until cooked.
4. Add the chicken broth to the diced chicken, and simmer.
5. Add the chopped celery into the saucepan.
6. Add the chopped green onions into the saucepan.
7. Prepare the zucchini noodles. You can use a potato peeler to make long strands or use other methods such as using a food processor (w/ shredding attachment) or spiralizer.
8. Add the zucchini noodles and the chopped cilantro into the pot.

9. Allow to simmer for a few more minutes. Dash with a pinch of salt to taste.

10. Transfer to a bowl and serve while hot. Enjoy!

Baby Zucchini Beef Burgers

Ingredients

- 1 pc. large-sized zucchini, chopped into ½" slices (makes around 14 to 16 slices)

- ½ lb. of ground beef

- ¼ avocado sliced into small pieces

- 2 Tbsp. avocado or olive oil for greasing the baking tray

- 2 tsp. of salt

- 1 Tbsp. of mustard

- 1 Tbsp. of Greek yogurt (store-bought)

Directions:

1. Preheat the oven to 400° F.

2. Grease the baking tray with avocado oil; sprinkle 1 tsp. of salt across the tray.

3. Put the slices of zucchini into the tray.

4. Make small balls out of the ground beef then press them into patties. You should be able to form 7 to 8 patties. Put the patties on the tray.

5. Put the baking tray in the oven and bake for around 15 minutes. If preferred, you can pan-fry the beef patties and zucchini in avocado oil or grill them, instead of baking.

6. Thinly slice the avocado into small pieces.

7. Using the zucchini slices as burger buns, assemble the baby/mini burgers. Place an avocado slice on each burger, then top with mustard and Greek yogurt.

Onion Coconut Broccoli Bacon Salad

Ingredients

- 1 lb. of broccoli florets

- 2 pcs. of large-sized or 4 pcs. of small-sized red onions, sliced

- 1 cup of coconut cream

- 20 bacon slices, cut into small pieces

- Salt, to taste

Instructions

1. Fry the bacon. Using the bacon fat, cook the onions.

2. Blanche the broccoli florets. If preferred, instead of blanching, you can boil them to soften or use them raw.

3. Toss the bacon, broccoli florets, and onions with the coconut cream. Dash with salt to taste.

4. Best served and consumed at room temperature.

Garlic Zucchini Beef

Ingredients

- 10 oz. of beef, sliced against the grain (if possible) into 1 to 2" strips
- 1 pc. of zucchini, sliced thinly into 1 to 2" long strips
- 3 cloves of garlic, minced or diced
- ¼ cup of cilantro, chopped
- Avocado oil for cooking (olive or coconut oil, if preferred)
- 2 Tbsp. gluten-free tamari sauce

Instructions

1. Heat 2 Tbsp. of avocado oil on high heat setting.
2. Put the beef strips into the pan. Sauté on high heat for a couple of minutes.
3. Once the beef browns, toss the zucchini strips in, and continue to sauté.
4. When the zucchini softens, add the garlic, cilantro, and tamari sauce.
5. Saute for a few more minutes.
6. Remove from heat and transfer into a plate.
7. Serve immediately.

Yummy Tuna Avocado Salad

Ingredients

- 4 oz. tuna (canned)
- 1 medium-sized egg, hard-boiled, peeled, & chopped
- ½ pc. of avocado
- ½ stalk of celery, diced
- 2 Tbsp. of mayonnaise
- ½ tsp. of fresh lemon juice
- 1 tsp. of mustard
- Salt & pepper to taste

Instructions

1. In a small-sized bowl, mix the tuna, celery, and avocado.
2. Stir in the mayonnaise, lemon juice, mustard, and spices and then add the chopped egg.
3. Mix everything well.
4. Serve and enjoy immediately, or if preferred, allow to cool in the refrigerator for up to an hour first.

Cauliflower Mushroom Risotto

Ingredients:

- 1 pound white mushrooms, thinly sliced

- 4 cups cauliflower florets

- 2 shallots, chopped

- 1 pound Portobello mushrooms, thinly sliced

- 3 tablespoons fresh chives, chopped

- 4 tablespoons butter

- Sea salt to taste

- Freshly ground black pepper to taste

- 3 tablespoons coconut oil or butter, divided

- 1/3 cup parmesan cheese, freshly grated

- ¼ cup vegetable broth

Directions:

1. Toss the cauliflower florets in the food processor bowl and pulse until you get a rice like grainy texture. If you don't want to pulse it, you can grate the cauliflower.

2. Heat a large saucepan or wok over medium high flame. Add about 2 tablespoons oil. When the oil starts heating, add the mushrooms and sauté until they become soft. Remove the mushrooms from heat and set aside.

3. Place a skillet over medium heat. Add remaining oil to it. When the oil is heated, add the shallots and sauté for about a minute. Add the cauliflower rice and sauté for another couple of minutes.

4. Add the vegetable broth and cook until the broth gets absorbed in the cauliflower rice. Transfer this mix in the wok.

5. Place the wok back on heat. Add butter, salt, pepper, chives and Parmesan. Mix it well until the risotto is well combined.

6. Serve hot.

Healthy Grain Free Low Carb Pizza Rolls

Ingredients:

- 2 tablespoon chopped onions
- ½ cup chopped red & green peppers
- ½ cup sausages, cooked & crumbled
- ¼ cup pizza sauce
- 2 cups mozzarella cheese
- 1 teaspoon pizza seasoning
- 1 -2 grape tomatoes, sliced

Directions:

1. Preheat your oven for 30 minutes at 400 degrees F
2. Line a large parchment paper in a baking pan. Slightly grease it with olive oil
3. Cover the parchment paper with the grated cheese without any gaps.
4. Season the cheese with pizza seasoning.

5. Stack it in the preheated oven to and bake at 400 F it until cheese turn brown and gets fully baked.

6. Take out from the oven and gently remove from the baking pan.

7. Garnish the cheese base with diced onions, crumbled sausages, both the bell peppers and sliced grape tomatoes.

8. Spread the tomato sauce on the pizza and sprinkle more pizza seasoning over it.

9. Toss it back in the oven for another 10 minutes, or until it is baked evenly on all sides.

10. Take it out of the oven and cut it into thick stripes and roll it up to form pizza rolls.

11. Serve when it is set.

Cheesy Mashed Cauliflower

Ingredients:

- 1 head cauliflower, made into small floret's

- ¼ cup cheddar cheese, shredded

- 1 tablespoon butter

- 2 tablespoons heavy cream

- Salt to taste

- Pepper to taste

Directions:

1. Toss the cauliflower florets in a microwave safe bowl along with half of the cream and butter.

2. Microwave the florets on high for 6 minutes (uncovered). Toss in the remaining butter and cream.

3. Mix it all well and microwave on high for another 6-7 minutes.

4. Keep stirring in between and when done, remove from microwave. Sprinkle the shredded cheese and blend the mix with a stick blender until smooth. You can also use a food processor.

5. Season with salt and pepper and serve.

Green Chilies Chicken

Ingredients:

- 2 boneless, skinless, chicken breast halves

- ½ cup whipped cream

- ½ cup chicken broth

- 4 ounces white onions (chopped finely)

- 3 ounces green chilies

- 3 ounces cans diced tomatoes

- 3 garlic cloves, minced

- ½ tsp. cayenne pepper

- 2 tbsp. butter

- ½ tsp. cumin

- ½ tsp. garlic powder

- Salt as per taste.

For garnish

- Sour cream

- Grated cheddar cheese

- Salsa

Directions:

- Wash the chicken breasts and slice them in vertical pieces.

- Heat a skillet on medium flame and melt the butter. Once the butter starts melting, add the onions and garlic to the skillet.

- Saute them till the onions turn golden brown and are translucent.

- Then add the sliced chicken to the skillet and sauté well. Once the chicken is cooked, add the tomatoes and chili. Mix it well and cover the skillet and let the mix cook for about twenty minutes.

- Once all the ingredients are cooked, add the cheese to the chicken and cook till the cheese melts. Now, add the cream and continue to mix the ingredients together.

- Pour the chicken broth to this mixture and sauté the ingredients well; let the liquid get soaked and dry.

- Garnish with all or either of the garnish' mentioned and serve hot.

Creamy Steak in Mushroom Sauce

Ingredients:

- 2 pound rib eye steak

- 10 ounce mushrooms

- 2 ounce heavy cream

- 1 tablespoon butter

- 4 ounces port wine

- Salt and Pepper to taste

Directions:

1. Season the steak with salt and pepper on both the sides.

2. Heat a cast iron skillet without a handle over high flame. Add the butter to the skillet, once it starts melting, add the steak and cook until the steak is cooked medium rare, or brown on both sides (it shouldn't take more than 2 minutes on each side for a medium-rare steak).

3. Take it off from heat and transfer into a baking tray lined with a foil.

4. Bake in a preheated oven at 450° F until the steak is cooked. Flip sides in between.

5. Remove from the oven and cover with foil. Keep the steak aside.

6. Heat the same skillet back again and pour the port wine, add the mushrooms and cream and let it simmer until the sauce thickens.

7. Pour the wine and mushroom sauce over the steak and serve hot.

Black Pepper Low Carb Beef Pie

Ingredients:

- 1 pounds extra lean ground beef

- ½ packet frozen vegetables

- 2 cups fresh cauliflower florets

- ¾ cup chicken broth

- ¾ cup beef broth

- 1 large yellow onion, chopped

- 2 cloves garlic, minced

- 1 teaspoon steak seasoning

- 1 teaspoon black pepper powder

- Sea salt to taste

- 1 teaspoon dried rosemary

Directions:

1. Boil a large pot of water and add a teaspoon of salt to it. Add the cauliflower florets to the boiling water and cook until tender. Once cooked, drain the water and keep it aside to cool.

2. Once cooled, mash the cauliflower well and set aside.

3. Heat a large skillet over medium flame and add the ground beef, onion and garlic and sauté well.

4. Keep stirring and cook the meat until it is browned and cooked. Once done, keep it aside.

5. Drain the excess fat in the meat mixture.

6. Add steak seasoning, salt and pepper, beef and chicken broth and frozen vegetables to the meat

7. Let it cook until the excess liquid dries up and the veggies are cooked.

8. Transfer this mix in a large baking dish.

9. Spread the mashed cauliflower mix over the meat mixture.

10. Toss the baking dish into a preheated oven at 350° F and bake for about 20 -30 minutes or till it becomes brown.

Macadamia Curried Tuna Balls

Ingredients

- 3 oz. of tuna in oil, drained
- 1 oz. of crumbled macadamia nuts
- 2 oz. of cream cheese
- ¼ tsp. of curry powder, divided

Directions:

1. Process the tuna, half of the curry powder, and cream cheese in a small-sized food processor. It should take about half a minute before the desired smooth and creamy consistency is achieved.

2. Form 6 balls from the mixture.

3. Place the remaining curry powder and crumbled macadamia nuts on a medium-sized plate.

4. Roll the balls individually to make sure each one is evenly coated.

5. Serve and enjoy immediately. If preferred, refrigerate first before serving, and use within 3 days.

Chapter 4 KETOGENIC DINNER

Delux Oven-Baked Rib-eye Steak

Ingredients:

3 medium rib-eye steaks

3 tablespoons butter

1 tablespoon paprika

1 tablespoon garlic powder

Pinch of salt and ground black pepper

Directions:

Rub the rib-eye steaks with salt, pepper, paprika and garlic powder. Place it in a lightly-greased baking dish. Bake the steaks in a 250°F oven for 45 minutes.

Use a cooking thermometer to check for the steak's doneness. If it reaches 120°F then the steak is ready. Remove the steak from the oven and let it stand for 5 minutes.

Heat the butter in a pan over medium flame. Once the oil is hot, place the steaks on the pan and sear each side of the meat for 30-40 seconds. Serve immediately.

Honey Chicken Breast with Citrus Sauce

Ingredients:

3 chicken breast halves, skin intact

2 cups kale leaves, washed and stems discarded

½ teaspoon butter

2 tablespoons heavy cream

3 tablespoons olive oil

2 tablespoons organic honey

½ teaspoon dried rosemary

1 cup fresh orange juice

Pinch of salt and ground black pepper

Directions:

Season the chicken breast with salt and pepper. Place it in a pan over medium-high flame and cook each side for 8-10 minutes. Set aside.

While the chicken breasts are cooking, heat the olive oil in a pan over medium flame. Add in the rosemary, orange juice and honey and simmer for 5-7 minutes. Pour in the heavy cream and cook for 3 minutes. Turn off the heat and set aside.

Place the butter and kale leaves on the same pan where the chicken breast was cooked. Cook the greens for 3-5 minutes or until the leaves wilt.

Transfer the wilted greens on a plate and arrange the chicken breasts on top of it. Pour the orange sauce on top of the dish. Serve immediately.

Coconut Crusted Chilli Shrimp

Ingredients:

450 grams shrimps, peeled and deveined

2 tablespoons coconut flour

1 cup dried coconut flakes

2 egg whites

1 red chili, minced

½ cup crushed pineapple

1 tablespoon lemon juice

1½ tablespoons white vinegar

Pinch of red pepper flakes

Directions:

Preheat the oven to 225°F and line a baking sheet with parchment paper.

Beat the egg whites until soft white peaks form. Set this aside. Place the coconut flour and coconut flakes in separate bowls.

Dip each shrimp in this order: coconut flour, egg whites then coconut flakes. Arrange the shrimps on the baking sheet until all seafood has been coated. Place the shrimps in the oven and bake for 5 minutes. Turn off the oven and arrange the shrimp on a serving platter.

To make the dip, mix together the crushed pineapple, lemon juice, vinegar and pepper flakes. Place the mixture in a sauce bowl and serve alongside the coconut shrimp.

Beef Noodles

- 5 to 6-ounce Cellophane noodles
- 1/3 cup Soy sauce
- 5 tablespoons Sesame oil
- 1 clove minced garlic
- 1/3 cup brown sugar
- 1 1/2 tablespoons apple vinegar
- 12 ounces skirt steak (1/4 inch thick slices)
- 1/4-inch wedges onion
- Kosher salt to taste
- 10 ounces Shiitake mushrooms (remove stems)
- 1 cup shredded carrots

- 6 cups baby spinach

Directions:

1. In the first step, you have to soak noodles in water (warm water) for almost 5 – 10 minutes. Drain water and snip noodle into pieces with kitchen scissors.
2. It is time to take a bowl and mix sesame oil (3 tablespoons), soy sauce, garlic, vinegar and brown sugar. Keep it aside. It is time to put beef to another and add two tablespoons soy sauce mixture. Keep it aside.
3. Take a large cooking pan and heat two teaspoons oil. Add salt and onion in this pan and cook for two minutes. Now, add beef and let it cook for a few minutes. Transfer beef in a bowl and keep it aside.
4. Rinse your cooking pan and heat two teaspoons oil again. Add carrots and mushroom and cook for three minutes. It is time to add noodles and two tablespoons soy sauce blend. Cook for one minute and add only 1/3 cup water and cook to make noodles tender. It will take almost three minutes. Transfer noodles in a bowl with beef.
5. Clean skillet again and keep it on the heat again and add remaining sesame oil. Add remaining mixture of soy sauce and spinach and cook them for one minute. It is time to add beef and mix them well.

Italian Style Turkey Meatballs

Ingredients:

- 1 lb. turkey meat, ground
- ½ cup mozzarella cheese, cut into bite sized cubes
- ½ cup grated Romano cheese
- 1 egg
- 5 garlic clove, minced
- 2 teaspoons fresh parsley, chopped
- 1 cup whole wheat panko bread

- ½ cup warm water
- 6 tablespoons olive oil
- 3 teaspoons Italian seasoning
- ½ teaspoon sugar
- 1 teaspoon salt
- ½ teaspoon red pepper flakes, crushed
- 1 can tomatoes, crushed
- 2 pinch of salt
- 1 pinch of pepper
- Salt and black pepper to taste

Directions:

1. Mix the turkey meat, egg, cheese, seasoning, parsley, half of the minced garlic, panko bread, salt and pepper. Mix well until you can shape it into meatballs

2. Preheat oven at 200 degrees Celsius.

3. Prepare a skillet over medium heat and add olive oil.

4. Use a tablespoon to scoop a piece of meat onto a baking sheet, place the cheese on top and cover it with another piece of meat. Roll the meat into meatballs.

5. Add the meatballs into your skillet to fry them. Fry the meatballs on all sides for about 1-2 minutes.

6. Take the meatballs out and place them back on the baking sheet to be baked in the oven for 10-12 minutes.

7. Add oil to your skillet pan over medium heat.

8. Add remaining garlic to be sautéed till golden.

9. Add the remaining ingredients (seasoning, pepper flakes, sugar, tomatoes, salt and pepper) to create your sauce. Simmer the mix for about 8 minutes. Add salt and pepper to taste.

10. By this time, your meatballs are ready to be added into the sauce mix.

Steak and Scramble Eggs

Ingredients:

- ½ cup lean sirloin steaks, cut into bite sized cubes
- 2 free range eggs
- 4 egg whites
- 2 teaspoons olive oil
- 1 medium potato, cut into bite sized cubes
- 1 teaspoon skim milk
- ¼ cup mushrooms
- 2 teaspoons Worcestershire sauce
- 2 tablespoons low-fat cheese, shredded
- 30 ml onions, chopped
- Paprika to taste
- Salt and black pepper to taste

Directions:

1. Heat a skillet pan over a medium-high heat.
2. Add oil, potatoes, onions, paprika and cook for 5 minutes. You may add salt and pepper to taste.
3. In a separate bowl, beat the eggs. Add milk as you continue to beat the egg.
4. Now, coming back to your pan, add Worcestershire sauce, mushrooms and the main dish, steak. Cook for about 4-6 minutes.
5. There will be excess fat from the pan mix. Drain the excess fat.
6. Add the eggs mix to the pan and scramble them together for about 4 minutes.
7. Once again, the dish is ready to serve. Sprinkle cheese to the dish and watch it melt just right.

Wheat-Free Chilli Pork and Veggie Sandwich

Ingredients:

900 grams lean ground pork
½ cup tomato sauce
1 large white onion, minced
2 eggs
Slices of tomato and cucumber
1½ tablespoons melted butter
½ teaspoon paprika
½ teaspoon chili powder
Pinch of salt and black pepper

Directions:

Place the chopped onions in a pan over medium-high heat then pour in the melted butter. Cook the onions for 3 minutes then let it cool.

In a large bowl, mix together the pork, tomato sauce, eggs and cooked onions. Season it with salt, pepper, chili powder and paprika then mix thoroughly. Divide the pork mixture into 6 patties and place them on a parchment-lined baking sheet. Bake the patties in a 350°F oven for 45 minutes.

Once the patties are cooked, remove it from the oven and allow them to cool. Slice each patty horizontally in the middle to make 2 loaves. Place a patty slice on a plate, top with cucumbers and tomatoes then cover it with the other patty. Serve immediately.

Coconut Honey Grilled Tilapia Fillet

Ingredients:

3 Tilapia fillets
2 tablespoons lime zest
1 teaspoon sea salt
1 tablespoon lemon pepper seasoning
1 teaspoon garlic powder
1 tablespoon melted coconut oil
2 cups arugula, washed and drained
1 tablespoon lemon juice
1 tablespoon olive oil
1 teaspoon honey

Directions:

To make the arugula salad, mix together the arugula leaves, lemon juice, olive oil and honey until the leaves are well-coated. Set this aside.

In another bowl, combine the lime zest, sea salt, lemon pepper seasoning and garlic powder. Place the tilapia fillets into the spice mixture and coat evenly.

Grease the grill pan with the coconut oil and place it over medium-high flame. Place the tilapia on the grill pan and cook each side for 3-5 minutes.

Once the fillets are cooked, arrange them on a serving plate. Serve the tilapia with the prepared arugula salad.

Garlic Mozzarella Meaty Pizza

Ingredients:

1 pound of beef (minced)

1 free range egg

1 1/2 cups of keto-friendly Marinara Sauce

1/2 teaspoon of powdered onion

1/2 teaspoon of powdered garlic

Salt and pepper to taste

1 teaspoon of oregano (dried)

1/4 cup of parmesan (grated)

15 slices of pepperoni

11/2 cups of mozzarella (shredded)

Directions:

Set your oven to 400°F. Mix together the egg and meat. Add in the parmesan and garlic and seasoning.

Cover the base of a pie plate, so that you have a crust. Bake for about twenty minutes or until the meat loses its pink tinge and is cooked through.

Take out of the oven and top with marinara sauce.

Top this with the mozzarella and the pepperoni.

Bake for another few minutes until the cheese has melted.

Onion Coconut Stir-Fried Pork

Ingredients:

1 medium-sized sweet onion

2 tablespoons of melted coconut oil

3 cloves of crushed garlic

1 pound of pork (finely ground)

1 big zucchini

10 ounces of spinach

1 cup of broccoli (cooked and chopped)

1 teaspoon of dried sage

1 teaspoon of garlic flakes

1 teaspoon of onion flakes

Salt and pepper to taste

1/2 teaspoon of flaked red pepper (omit if you don't like spicy food)

1 big avocado (cubed)

Directions:

Set your stove to medium-high.

Fry the garlic and onion in the coconut oil until softened and transparent. Add in the zucchini and fry until softened.

Fry the pork until all traces of pink are gone. Once the meat is done, add in the spinach and allow it to wilt.

Add in all the remaining ingredients except the avocado and heat through.

Divide into four equal portions, top with the avocado, and serve.

Bacon Crusted Stuffing

Ingredients:

4 medium-sized bell peppers (green peppers have the lowest carb count)

1/2 cup of mild onion (chopped)

1 tablespoon of good quality olive oil

1 pound of beef (finely ground)

4 rashers of bacon (cubed)

2 cloves of crushed garlic

1 big tomato (cubed)

2 teaspoons of dried Italian seasoning

1/2 cup of cheddar (shredded)

1/2 cup of mozzarella (shredded)

1/4 cup of keto-friendly Marinara sauce

Directions:

Set your oven to 375°F. Take the top third off the pepper and deseed them. Put to one side. Set your stove to medium.

Fry the garlic and onion in the heated olive oil until they become transparent. Brown the ground beef. Add the tomato, bacon, and seasoning and mix well. Add the marinara sauce.

Divide the mixture evenly and stuff the peppers. Stand them in an oven-proof dish upright, and bake for about fifty minutes. The meat should reach a temperature of 165°F.

Turn on the broiler and sprinkle the peppers with cheese.

Allow to broil for a few minutes until the cheese starts to bubble and the peppers start charring. Serve immediately.

Hot Sauce Bacon Cheese Burgers

Ingredients:

1 pound of beef (finely ground)
3 tablespoons of onion (finely chopped)
1/3 cup of double cream
1 clove of crushed garlic
1/8 teaspoon of hot sauce (can be left out)
Salt and pepper to taste
4 slices of cheddar
4 rashers of bacon
1 sliced avocado
2 tablespoons of Keto-friendly Mayo

Directions:

Put on the broiler. Mix well together the beef, cream, seasoning, onion, and garlic. Divide into four evenly sized patties and broil for around four minutes per side or till cooked to your liking.

Turn oven on to broil. Put a piece of cheese on each burger and broil for a little while longer until the cheese melts.

Add the bacon and avocado, put on mayo to taste, and serve.

Rosemary Thyme Cottage Pie

Ingredients:

2 celery stalks (finely diced)

1 1/2 pounds of lamb (finely ground)

3 cloves of crushed garlic

1 medium-sized onion (finely diced)

1 medium-sized zucchini (finely diced)

2 tablespoons of coconut oil

1 teaspoon of rosemary (dried)

1 teaspoon of thyme (dried)

Salt and pepper to taste

1/2 teaspoon of powdered garlic

3 tablespoons of farm butter

4 cups of cooked cauliflower

1/4 cup of double cream

1/2 teaspoon of garlic salt

3/4 cup of cheddar (shredded)

Directions:

Set the oven to 350°F. Fry the garlic and onions in the oil until translucent. Fry the zucchini and celery until softened.

Add the ground lamb and seasoning, and cook until browned. Put the meat into an oven-proof dish and set aside. Process the cauliflower, butter, and cream until smooth. Layer on top of the ground lamb and sprinkle the cheese over that. Bake for around half an hour until heated through, and allow to stand for a few minutes before you serve it.

Yummy Heavy Cream Garlic Fried Hake Fillet

Ingredients

- 10 oz. hake filets
- 1+ 1 tbsp. coconut oil
- ¼ onion, minced
- 2 cloves garlic
- 16 oz. spinach
- ⅓ cup heavy cream
- salt and pepper

Directions:

1. Heat 1 tbsp. coconut oil in a large frying pan. Add the hake, skin side down, and cook for 5-6 minutes. Flip and cook for another 3-4 minutes until the flesh is opaque throughout.
2. Meanwhile, heat 1 tbsp. coconut oil in a medium frying pan. Add the onions and garlic and cook for 2-3 minutes. Add the spinach and cook just until wilted.
3. Add the cream to the spinach and season with salt and pepper. Simmer for 2 minutes more until the cream thickens. Serve the hake with the spinach on the side.

Coconut Caramelized Onions Baked Hake Fillet

Ingredients

- 2 onions, thinly sliced
- 2 + 2 tbsp. coconut oil, melted
- 10 oz. hake filets
- 1 cup cherry tomatoes
- salt and pepper

Directions:

1. In a large pan, heat 2 tbsp. coconut oil and add the onions. Cook over medium heat, stirring frequently, until they are golden brown and reduced greatly, about 30 minutes.
2. Meanwhile, lay the hake filets in a baking pan lined with parchment paper. Toss the cherry tomatoes with 2 tbsp. coconut oil and add them to the pan. Use a spoon to spread any excess oil onto the fish.
3. Bake the fish and tomatoes for 15-20 minutes at 350°F until the hake is opaque and flakes easily.
4. Serve with the caramelized onions.

Garlic Coconut Almond Crusted Tilapia

Ingredients

- 10 oz. tilapia filets
- ¼ cup ground almonds
- ¼ cup shredded coconut
- 2 tbsp. coconut oil, melted
- 1 clove garlic, minced

- 1 tsp. lime zest
- salt and pepper
- 1½ cups green beans
- 2 tbsp. slivered almonds
- 1 tbsp. butter

Directions:

1. Lay the tilapia on a baking sheet.
2. Mix the ground almonds, coconut, coconut oil, garlic, lime zest, salt, and pepper together and spread evenly over the fish.
3. Bake for 15-20 minutes at 350°F until the tilapia is opaque and the crust is crunchy.
4. Meanwhile, steam the green beans in the microwave or on the stove top until bright green. Toss with the butter and slivered almonds and serve with the tilapia.

Zested Butter Rainbow Trout

Ingredients

- 10 oz. rainbow trout filets
- 1 recipe <u>Avocado Dressing</u>
- 1 tsp. lemon zest
- 2 tbsp. butter, melted

Directions:

1. Pat the filets dry with paper towel and brush both sides with melted butter. Broil for 4-6 minutes until fish is opaque and flakes easily.
2. Meanwhile, make the avocado dressing, adding 1 tsp. lemon zest.
3. Serve the fish warm with the avocado sauce on the side.

Sour Cream Baked Fish Fillet

Ingredients

- 10 oz. Arctic char filet
- 2 tbsp. mayonnaise
- ½ cup sour cream
- 3 tbsp. thinly sliced chives
- 2 cups steamed broccoli (serve on the side)

Directions:

1. Lay the Arctic char skin side down on a baking sheet. Use the back of a spoon to spread the mayonnaise over the top; this helps keep the fish moist while baking.
2. Bake at 400°F for 10-13 minutes, until the fish is opaque and flakes easily.
3. Serve fish topped with sour cream and chives and steamed broccoli on the side.

Delicious Coconut Fish Curry

Ingredients

- 1 tbsp. coconut oil
- ½ onion, chopped

- 1 red pepper, chopped
- 3 cloves garlic, minced
- ½ inch ginger, minced
- 1 15 oz. can coconut milk
- 2 tbsp. lime juice
- 1 tbsp. curry paste
- 8 oz. hake, in 4-5 pieces.
- handful fresh cilantro, roughly chopped

Directions:

1.   Heat the coconut oil in a large pan and add the onions and red pepper. Cook for 3 minutes or so, then add the garlic and ginger and cook for 2-3 minutes.

2.   Stir the coconut milk, lime juice, and curry paste together and pour into the pan. Bring to a simmer and add the hake. Cover and cook gently for 6-9 minutes, until the fish is opaque and flakes easily.

3.   Ladle the curry into bowls and serve with fresh cilantro.

Seared Scallops with Lemon Juice

Ingredients:

2 tsp canola oil

3 oz sea scallops

2 tsp lemon juice

1/2 tsp ground sage

1 1/2 cups cubed roasted acorn squash

2 cups kale sautéed in 2 tsp olive oil

Directions:

Warm canola oil in a huge nonstick skillet over high warmth
Include scallops and cook without mixing until all around seared, around two minutes. Flip scallops and cook until the sides are firm and focuses misty, 30 to 90 seconds. Shower with lemon squeeze, and sprinkle sage on top. Present with squash and kale.

Olive Oil Cheesy Veggie Pasta

Ingredients:
- 1/2 cup whole-wheat macaroni
- 1 cup crushed whole, peeled canned tomatoes
- 1/2 cup low-fat ricotta cheese
- 3/4 cup chopped spinach
- 1 cup zucchini wedges
- 2 tsp olive oil

Directions:
Cook vegetables over medium-high heat and combine with cooked macaroni & cheese.

Delicious Teriyaki Beef with Veggies

Ingredients:

- 3 oz grass-fed beef tenderloin, cubed

- 2 Tbsp reduced-sodium teriyaki sauce
- 1 Tbsp light honey-mustard dressing
- 2 tsp olive oil
- 1/4 cup sliced carrots
- 1/2 cup chopped broccoli
- 1/4 cup sliced water chestnuts
- 1/4 cup sliced peppers
- 1/2 cup cooked brown rice

Directions:

Marinate hamburger in teriyaki and dressing for 30 minutes.

Warm olive oil in a skillet, and cook meat one to two minutes. Include veggies, and cook for another five to seven minutes until hamburger is seared. Serve over rice.

Coconut Cheesy Chili Beef

Ingredients

- 2 + 2 tbsp. coconut oil
- 1 large onion, chopped
- 2 green peppers, seeded and chopped
- 3 cloves garlic, minced
- 12 oz. 80% lean ground beef
- 2 cups water
- 1 15 oz. can diced tomatoes
- 1 tbsp. cocoa powder
- 2 tsp. Worcestershire sauce
- 1 tsp. oregano
- 1-2 tsp. chili powder
- salt and pepper

- ½ cup sour cream
- ½ cup shredded cheddar cheese
- green onions, thinly sliced

Directions:

1. Heat 2 tbsp. coconut oil in a large skillet. Add the onions, peppers, and garlic and cook until softened.
2. Meanwhile, heat 2 tbsp. coconut oil in a soup pot. Add the ground beef and cook until browned.
3. Add the peppers, onions, tomatoes, water, cocoa powder, Worcestershire sauce oregano, chili powder, salt, and pepper to the pot with the beef. Simmer, covered, for about 2 hours. Add more water if needed.
4. Serve with cheese, sour cream, and green onions.

Zucchini Noodles Beef Lasagna

Ingredients
- 4 medium zucchini, very thinly sliced lengthwise on a mandoline
- 1 tbsp. + 2 tbsp. olive oil
- 1 onion, finely chopped
- 3 cloves garlic, minced
- 1½ lbs. 80% lean ground beef
- 3 tomatoes, chopped
- ½ each dried thyme, oregano, and basil
- 3 cups shredded mozzarella
- 1 cup grated parmesan
- salt and pepper

Directions:

1. Heat a large frying pan and add 1 tbsp. olive oil. Cook the zucchini slices for 2 minutes per side, until softened. Allow to drain on paper towels, pressing gently to remove excess moisture.
2. Heat 2 tbsp. olive oil in the frying pan and add the onion and garlic. Cook until softened and fragrant, 6-7 minutes, then add the ground beef.
3. Brown thoroughly, then add the chopped tomato and herbs. Cook until the tomatoes have softened and formed a sauce, about 10 minutes. Add salt and pepper to taste.
4. Lay⅓of the zucchini slices in the bottom of a medium casserole dish. Spread⅓of the ground beef mixture over it and sprinkle with 1 cup mozzarella and⅓ cup parmesan. Repeat this layering three times.
5. Bake for 20-30 minutes at 350°F until the cheese is melted and the sauce is bubbling.

Garlic Italian Sausage

Ingredients

- 3 tbsp. olive oil
- 4 sweet bell peppers – mix of colors
- 1 onion
- 3 cloves garlic
- 2 tsp. Italian seasoning
- 2 lbs. sweet Italian sausage, sliced

Directions:

1. Heat the olive oil in a large pan and add the peppers, onion, and garlic. Cook for 4-5 minutes, until fragrant and tender. Add the Italian seasoning and remove from pan.

2. Add the sausage to the pan and cook thoroughly, 10-12 minutes. Return the peppers to the pan and mix everything together. Serve.

Crispy Bacon Burgers

Ingredients

- ½ lb. 80% lean ground beef
- 1 tsp. Worcestershire sauce
- 2 slices cheddar cheese
- 4 strips crispy bacon
- 2 slices red onion
- ½ head butter or Bibb lettuce
- 1 avocado, sliced
- 1 tomato, sliced
- 1 large dill pickle, sliced
- mustard to taste

Directions:

1. Mix the ground beef with the Worcestershire sauce and form into two patties. Grill or pan fry over medium until no pink remains in the center, 5-7 minutes per side.
2. When the burgers are almost done, lay a slice of cheese on top and allow to melt.
3. Divide the lettuce between two plates and set the burgers on top. Top with red onion, avocado, tomato, bacon, pickle, and mustard.

Keto Delux Beef Stew

Ingredients

- 3 tbsp. coconut oil
- 1 lb. high-fat beef stew meat, such as chuck, cut into 1" pieces
- 1 onion, chopped
- ¼ lb. carrots, chopped
- ¼ lb. parsnips, chopped
- 4 cloves garlic, chopped
- handful fresh parsley
- salt and pepper
- ½ tsp. thyme
- 2 bay leaves
- 2 tsp. Worcestershire sauce
- 1 cup Guinness stout
- 1 qt. beef broth

Directions:

1. Heat the coconut oil in a soup pot and add the beef. Brown, then add the rest of the ingredients.
2. Simmer for 1½ - 2 hours until the beef is tender and the broth is thickened, adding more water as needed.

Shrimp Macaroni Pasta Salad

Ingredients:
- 4 oz cooked shrimp
- 1/2 cup cooked whole-wheat elbow macaroni
- 1/2 steamed broccoli
- 4 sun-dried tomatoes, halved
- 1 tsp capers
- 2 Tbsp red wine vinegar
- 1/4 tsp onion powder
- 1/2 tsp oregano

Directions:
Toss all ingredients together, and serve cold.

Parmesan Spinach Chicken with Penne

Ingredients:

- 4 oz grilled chicken, diced
- 1/2 cup tomato sauce
- 1 cup spinach
- 1/2 cup whole-wheat penne
- 1 1/2 Tbsp grated Parmesan

Directions:

Sauté spinach in one teaspoon olive oil, & hurl with chicken, penne, & tomato sauce. Beat with Parmesan.

Butternut Squash Soup Stir-FryBeef

Ingredients:
- 3 oz steak tenderloin fillet, sliced thin
- 1/2 cup sliced shiitake mushrooms
- 1/2 onion, sliced
- 2 tsp olive oil
- 1/3 cup cooked bulgur

Butternut Squash Soup
- 1/2 cup Pacific Natural Foods organic light-sodium
- Stir-fry beef, onion, & mushroom.
- Asian Snapper
- 1/4 cup raw pistachios
- 1/2 cup cooked millet
- 1/2 cup bok choy
- 6 oz cooked snapper
- 4 tsp low-sodium soy sauce
- 2 tsp sesame seeds
- 1/2 cup sugar snap peas, cooked

Directions:

Blend pistachios into millet.
Beat millet with bok choy and after that snapper.

Shower snapper with soy sauce, and sprinkle with sesame seeds. Serve sugar snap peas as an afterthought.

Yummy Rosemary Parsley Cod Polenta and Beans

Ingredients:

- 3 oz cod
- 1 tsp chopped fresh parsley
- Dash of salt
- Dash of pepper
- 1/4 cup dry polenta
- 1/2 cup 1 percent milk
- 1 Tbsp pine nuts
- 1/2 tsp rosemary
- 1/2 cup cooked green beans

Directions:

Season cod with parsley, salt, and pepper, then steam for eight minutes.

Cook polenta with drain, per bundle guidelines, and after that top with pine nuts and rosemary.

Present with green beans.

Tasty Roast Beef Wrap

Ingredients:

- 2 Tbsp 2% plain Greek yogurt
- 1 Tbsp horseradish sauce
- 2 leaves Bibb lettuce
- 4 slices lean deli-style roast beef
- 4 slices tomato
- 1 cup fresh raspberries

Directions:

Join yogurt and horseradish, and spread on lettuce.
Best with dish meat and tomato, and move into a wrap.
Top with raspberries.

Onion Tuna-Avocado Sandwich

Ingredients:

- 1/3 avocado, mashed
- 1/2 Tbsp lemon juice
- 4 oz white albacore tuna, drained
- 1 thick slice tomato
- 1 piece butter lettuce
- 1 slice red onion
- 1 slice whole-grain bread

Directions:

Join avocado with lemon squeeze, and overlay in fish. Stack tomato, lettuce, onion, and avocado and fish blend on bread for an open-confront sandwich.

Slow Cooker Roast Beef with Honey Citrus Sauce

Ingredients:

900 grams beef chuck roast
2 tablespoons fresh lime juice
2 tablespoons fresh orange juice
1 tablespoon honey
½ cup olive oil
3 garlic cloves, minced
½ cup chopped cilantro
1 large shallot, minced
1 teaspoon chili powder
2 teaspoons oregano powder
2 teaspoons sea salt
¼ teaspoon cumin
¼ teaspoon coriander
¼ cup water

Directions:

Place the beef chuck inside the slow cooker. Let it stand for 20-30 minutes.

In a food processor, mix together the lime juice, orange juice, honey, olive oil, cilantro, shallot, chili powder, oregano, salt, cumin and coriander. Pour the mixture into the pot, making sure to coat the beef evenly. Pour in the water then cover the pot.

Set the temperature to high and cook the beef for 4 hours, turning the meat every hour. After 4 hours, turn off the slow cooker and tilt the cover of the pot to let the heat dissipate. Leave it for 20 minutes.

Remove the beef from the pot and place it on a serving plate. Slice the meat according to preferred thickness and pour the citrus sauce over it. Serve immediately.

Garlic Coconut Fish Fingers

Ingredients:

450 grams cream dory, sliced into strips

¾ cup shredded coconut

2 medium eggs, beaten

4 tablespoons olive oil

Pinch of salt and black pepper

For the Dip:

1 teaspoon garlic powder

3 tablespoons mayonnaise

½ teaspoon honey

Directions:

Wash the fish strips and drain completely. Place the eggs in a bowl and put the shredded coconut on a separate plate.

Heat the olive oil in a pan over medium high flame.

Dip the fish finger into the egg mixture then roll it on the grated coconut. Repeat this procedure again to ensure that the fish is evenly coated.

Place the fish finger into the pan and cook until the sides have turned golden brown. Lay the fish finger on a wire rack to cool. Arrange the fish fingers on a serving plate and serve immediately.

For the dip, mix together the mayonnaise, garlic powder and honey. Pour the mixture in a sauce bowl and serve.

Onion Sage Turkey Burgers

Ingredients
- 1½ pounds ground turkey
- ½ small onion, minced
- 1 tsp. dried sage
- 1 egg
- salt and pepper
- 2 tbsp. butter

Directions:

1. Mix first five ingredients and form into four patties.
2. Heat a large skillet and add butter.

Add the burgers and cook until well browned on the outside and no pink remains on the inside, 6-7 minutes per side. Serve.

Zucchini Noodles and Meatballs

Ingredients:

2 big zucchini
2 tablespoons of good quality olive oil
1 cup of onion (diced)
2 cloves of crushed garlic
1 egg
½ cup of cheddar (grated)
Seasoning to taste
½ teaspoon of chili flakes
½ pound each of ground beef and pork
2 tablespoons of butter
2 cups of homemade marinara sauce

Directions

Preheat oven to 375° F.

Slice zucchini into wafer-thin strips with a potato peeler. Lay the strips out onto an absorbent towel, so that they can sweat.

Heat up the oil in a big pan and add garlic and onions. Fry till softened and set aside.

Mix cheddar, egg, seasoning, and the meat in a big bowl. Add garlic and onions and mix again.

Divide mixture into 12 evenly sized balls and bake for around 20 minutes.

Melt butter over medium heat and fry zucchini strips until just soft. Serve with meatballs and a helping of marinara sauce.

Tasty Five Spice Chicken

Ingredients

- 1 ½ pounds chicken leg quarters
- 2 cloves garlic, minced
- 1 inch piece ginger, grated
- 2 teaspoons five spice powder
- 1 medium onion, finely chopped
- 2 tablespoons fresh cilantro
- ½ cup chicken broth
- Salt to taste
- Pepper to taste

Directions:

1. Place the chicken legs in a pot. Pour the broth over it. Sprinkle, garlic, ginger and onions over it. Finally sprinkle five-spice powder, salt and pepper.
2. Let the mixture simmer until it gets well cooked.
3. Serve hot.

Chili Coconut Chicken Bake

Ingredients

- 2 tbsp. coconut oil
- 2 large mild green chilies, such as poblano, seeded and chopped
- 1 small onion, chopped
- 4 cloves garlic, minced
- 2 large tomatoes, chopped
- ½ cup canned chipotle chilies in adobo sauce
- Meat from 4 chicken thighs, cooked and chopped into bite-size pieces

- 2 cups shredded cheddar cheese
- 1 cup sour cream
- 1 handful fresh cilantro, roughly chopped

Directions:

1.   Heat the coconut oil in a large pan. Cook the green chilies, onions, and garlic for 5 minutes, then add the tomatoes. Cook until very soft, about ten minutes.
2.   Turn off the heat and stir in the chicken, chipotle peppers, and half the cheese.
3.   Pour into a small casserole pan and top with the remaining cheese. Bake for 30 minutes at 350°F, until the cheese is melty and bubbling. Serve with sour cream and cilantro.

Turkey and Vegetable Pot Pie

Ingredients:

1 cup leftover turkey meat, diced
1 egg, beaten
1 cup diced celery
1 cup diced zucchini
1 cup homemade chicken broth
Pinch of salt and ground black pepper
For the Crust:
2 large eggs
½ cup coconut oil
1½ cups almond flour
½ cup coconut flour
Pinch of sea salt

Directions:

To make the crust, combine the almond and coconut flours in a bowl then season it with salt. Add in coconut oil and egg. Knead through the mixture until a soft dough forms.

Separate the dough mixture into 2 balls. Place each dough ball in between 2 sheets of wax paper then use a rolling pin to flatten them. Place one flattened dough in a lightly-greased pie pan and spread the dough until the sides of the pan are covered. Bake this in a 325°F oven for 6-8 minutes.

While the pie crust is baking, place the turkey, egg, celery, zucchini and chicken broth in a saucepan and simmer over medium flame for 8 minutes. Season it with salt and pepper. Once the liquids have reduced, turn off the heat and set aside.

Once the pie crust is ready, remove it from the oven and let it cool for 3-5 minutes. Pour the turkey mixture into the pie crust. Slowly put the remaining flattened dough on top of the pie. Make sure to seal the sides of the pie but do make small vents on top by poking it with a fork or knife.

Place the pie in the oven and bake for 45-50 minutes. Slice into equal portions and serve.

Spinach Chili Beef Bowl

Ingredients:

900 grams ground beef

7 cups spinach leaves

1 green bell pepper, deseeded and chopped

1 red bell pepper, deseeded and chopped

1 medium onion, chopped

1 cup tomato sauce

1 tablespoon chili powder

1 tablespoon cumin

2 teaspoons cayenne pepper

1 teaspoon garlic powder

½ teaspoon curry powder

1 tablespoon olive oil

2 tablespoons cottage cheese

Pinch of salt and ground black pepper

Directions:

Place the ground beef in a pot and start cooking it over high flame. Stir every few minutes to prevent it from burning.

While the beef starts to cook, heat the olive oil in a large pan over medium flame. Add in the onions and bell peppers and sauté for 10 minutes. Add in the spinach leaves and cook for 10 more minutes. Season with salt and pepper and set aside.

Season the beef with chili powder, cumin, cayenne pepper, garlic powder and curry powder. Lower the flame to medium and continue cooking for 20-25 minutes.

Once the beef is cooked, add the cooked vegetables and tomato sauce into the pot and mix well. Simmer for 10 minutes then turn off the heat. Sprinkle some cottage cheese on top and serve while hot.

Delicious Stir Fry vegetable Beef

Ingredients

- 1 lb. beef
- 2 tbsp. coconut oil
- 1 cup onion minced
- 2 cups broccoli chopped
- 1 tbsp. sesame seeds
- 3 tbsp. green onion chopped
- 1 cup chestnuts sliced

Directions:

1.   First, clean the beef and cut it into small pieces of equal size.

2.   Place a pan over medium flame. Add the coconut oil to the pan and wait for it to heat.

3.   Once the coconut oil is hot, you will need to put the beef in the pan.

4.   Cook the beef and make sure that it is brown on all sides.

5.   Remove the beef from the pan and set it aside.

6.   Add the onion and the broccoli to the pan and sauté for a few minutes. You need to make sure that the onion is translucent and that the broccoli begins to wilt.

7.   Add the beef to the pan and fry for a few minutes. Once the flavors bend together. You could add more vegetables to the dish if you like.

Mozzarella Cheesy Stuffed Chicken

Ingredients:

- 4 boneless and skinless chicken breast
- ½ bottle garlic and herb marinade
- Fresh basil leaves
- 2 tomatoes (sliced)
- 4 slices mozzarella cheese
- 12 slices bacon

Directions:

1.   Slice chicken breast horizontally and pour marinade over chicken with breasts opened

2.   Let it sit for 30 minutes

3. In the meantime, preheat oven to 400 degrees F
4. Place chicken into pan and cover the chicken with enough tomatoes
5. Place cheese on chicken and fold the chicken over and hold with toothpick
6. Wrap 3 slices bacon around each breast
7. Cook for 20 minutes
8. Turn and cook chicken for 15 more minutes

Healthy Beef stew and leeks

Ingredients:

- 1 pound ground beef
- 2 cups chopped leeks
- 2 cups diced carrots
- 2 cups chopped onions
- 1 tsp. dried sage
- 1 cup chopped beans
- 1 cup chopped tomatoes
- 1 cup chopped mushrooms
- 1 cup chopped zucchini
- 1 cup cubed sweet potato
- 1 tsp. oregano
- 1 tbsp. olive oil
- 3 cups water
- Salt and pepper to taste

Directions:

1. Add oil to a skillet placed on medium flame and sauté the onions until they have turned golden brown.
2. Add the ground beef to the pan and cook until the beef has browned.

3. Now, add the remaining ingredients to the pan and continue to cook until you obtain a thick mixture.
4. Add the leeks to the pan and continue to cook until they have softened.
5. When the ingredients start to boil, cover the pan and simmer for a while.
6. Serve hot.

Mouth Watering Pizza

Ingredients
- 2 tbsp. olive oil
- 1 cauliflower head (trim and then chop the head into smaller pieces)
- 1 ounce white onion (minced)
- 3 tbsp. butter
- ½ cup water
- 4 eggs (2 large eggs)
- 3 cups mozzarella cheese (shredded and chopped into smaller pieces)
- 2 tsp. fennel seeds
- 3 tsp. Italian seasoning
- ½ cup parmesan (grated)
- 5 ounces Pizza Sauce (pick a sauce that is very low in carbohydrates)
- 1 pound Italian sausage (look for the sausage that has a very low amount of carbohydrates)
- 1 cup Italian cheese (preferably get the five cheese blend. You will have to shred the cheese.)

Directions:

For the crust

1. Preheat the oven to 400 degrees Fahrenheit.
2. Take a cookie sheet and grease it well with the olive oil.
3. Take a large skillet and place it on a medium flame.
4. Add the butter to the skillet and add the onions to the skillet and sauté them until they are translucent. Add the cauliflower to the skillet and cook it until it is almost done.
5. Add water to the skillet and cover the skillet. Leave the vegetables in until the cauliflower is cooked and soft.
6. Transfer the vegetables to a glass bowl and leave them to cool.
7. As the cauliflower is cooling, you will need to cook the Italian sausages. You will need to break them into smaller pieces and cook them well. Drain all the fat out from the skillet. Pat the sausages dry on a tissue paper to remove any excess fat. Leave these aside to cool.
8. Once the cauliflower has cooled down, take three cups of the cauliflower and place it in a food processor or a blender. You will need to blend it until the cauliflower has turned into a smooth puree. Move the puree into a mixing bowl.
9. Add the eggs to the mixing bowl along with the cheese and the spices. Blend them well. Now add the Parmesan cheese and mix it well!
10. Add the cauliflower puree to the cookie sheet and spread it neatly with a spatula. You will have to have a certain thickness all around the sheet.
11. Bake the crust in the oven for twenty minutes. Remove the crust when you find that it has turned brown at the edges.
12. While the pizza crust is in the oven, you will need to chop the sausages into fine pieces. You could either cut the sausage or process it in the food processor.
13. Pour the pizza sauce in a saucepan and add the Italian sausage to the pan.
14. Cook the sausage in the pizza sauce until the sauce has become thick.

For the pizza

1. Once the crust is cooked, you can remove it from the oven and turn the oven settings to boil. Leave the oven shelf four inches from the broiler.
2. Pour the sausage and sauce mixture over the crust. Spread the mixture over the crust using a spatula. You will have a thin coating of the sauce and the sausage. You could add more sausage and sauce to the crust if you want.

3. Leave the pizza in the oven and broil it until the cheese melts. You have to ensure that the cheese has begun to bubble.
4. Remove the pizza from the oven and cut how many ever slices you want.

Garlic Bacon Chuck Roast Stew

Ingredients

- 1 cup bacon strips
- 3 pounds chuck roast, fat trimmed
- 2 large red onions, sliced
- 2 minced garlic cloves
- 1 ½ teaspoon sea salt
- 1 teaspoon freshly ground black pepper
- 5 cups beef broth
- 1 teaspoon thyme
- 1 tablespoon olive oil
- Some chopped parsley for garnish

Method

1. Using a sharp knife, slice up the roast into thin pieces or small 2-inch chunks.
2. Heat tablespoon of olive oil over medium heat in a large saucepan.
3. Add the onion slices to it and sauté for 3 to 4 minutes until they start releasing water.
4. Now add the minced garlic and cook for another minute.

5. Pour some beef broth into the pan and sprinkle some salt, thyme and pepper on top. Stir all the ingredients well using a large wooden spoon.

6. Slide in the chuck roast chunks, bacon slices and cover the pan with a lid. Cook the stew for about 90 minutes on high flame and then let it simmer for another 15-20 minutes. If you are using a slow cooker, cook on low heat for 7 hours until the roast is completely cooked.

7. Transfer in a large plate and garnish with some chopped parsley on top.

8. Serve hot.

Butter Rosemary Chicken Thighs

Ingredients:

- 6 chicken thighs
- 1 1/2 lemons
- 3 cloves garlic
- 6 sprigs rosemary
- Salt to taste
- Pepper powder to taste
- 3 tablespoons butter

Directions:

1. Sprinkle chicken with salt and pepper.

2. Place a cast iron skillet over high heat. Place chicken thighs over the skillet. With its skin side down and cook until brown. Flip sides and brown the other side too. Sprinkle a little lemon juice over it. Chop the remaining lemon and add it to the pan and sauté.

3. Add garlic and rosemary and sauté.

4. Transfer the skillet into a preheated oven and bake at 400 degrees F for about 30 minutes.

5. Remove from oven and add butter and bake until crisp. Discard the lemon pieces.
6. Serve with sautéed vegetables.

The Best Chicken soup

Ingredients:

- 13 oz chicken breast, skinned, boneless
- 1.4 oz white onion
- 2.5 oz green beans
- ¼ cup almond milk
- 5 cups water
- ¼ cup cream cheese
- 5.3 oz zucchini
- 1 garlic clove
- 1 teaspoon salt
- ½ tablespoon dill

Directions:

1. Chop the chicken breast roughly and sprinkle it with salt.
2. Add dill and mix up the mixture with the help of the hands.
3. After this, pour water into the saucepan and toss chicken mixture.
4. Close the lid and cook it for 15 minutes.
5. Meanwhile, peel the onion and chop it.
6. Combine the chopped onion and green beans together. Mix it up.

7.   After this, chop the zucchini and add it to the chicken mixture.

8.   Cook it for 5 minutes more.

9.   Then add chopped onion mixture, cream cheese, and almond milk.

10.   Add garlic clove and cook the soup for 10 minutes on the medium heat.

11.   When the soup is cooked – stir it carefully with the help of the spoon and serve it immediately.

12.   Enjoy!

Meatballs Spaghetti Squash Lasagna

Ingredients:

- 5 cups roasted spaghetti squash (about 3)
- 2 cups parmesan cheese, grated
- 4 cups mozzarella cheese, shredded
- 2 pounds ground beef
- 1 teaspoon basil
- 2 teaspoon chili powder
- 1 teaspoon oregano
- 6 cloves garlic, peeled
- Sea salt to taste
- Pepper powder to taste
- 2 teaspoons red pepper flakes
- 3 cups low carb marinara sauce
- 2 eggs
- 2 tablespoons ghee or coconut oil

Directions:

1.   Preheat the oven to 350 F.

2.   Peel spaghetti squash (about 3 medium sized), deseed it and chop into chunks. Roast it in the oven at 350 degrees F for about an hour. Then measure 5 cups of spaghetti squash and mash it slightly. Or you can roast the squash without chopping it. Peel, deseed and mash after roasting it.

3.   Mince garlic and set aside

4.   Add marinara sauce and red pepper flakes to a pan, cover and simmer for 5 minutes.

5.   To make meat balls: Add ground beef, basil, chili powder, garlic, oregano, salt, pepper, and eggs to large bowl and mix well using your hands.

6.   Make small meatballs of the mixture with moistened hands.

7.   Place a frying pan over medium heat. Add about a tablespoon of ghee. When ghee melts, add around half the meatballs (do not crowd, fry it in batches).

8.   Flip sides and cook on all sides until brown. Remove the meatballs and set aside on a plate.

9.   Repeat with the remaining meatballs.

10.   Take a baking dish. Spread about ¾ cup marinara sauce. Next spread half the spaghetti squash over it followed by few meatballs.

11.   Next layer with Parmesan cheese followed by another layer of sauce followed by spaghetti squash.

12.   Next place a few meatballs. Sprinkle half the mozzarella cheese over it. Finally layer with the remaining sauce followed by spaghetti squash, meatballs and finally mozzarella cheese.

13.   Bake in a preheated oven at 350 for 30 minutes.

Garlic Kebab Chicken

Ingredients:

- Almonds (handful)

- 6 jalapeno peppers (chopped and seeded)
- 8 cloves of garlic
- 1 cup fresh cilantro (chopped)
- Pinch of salt
- Juice of one lemon
- ½ cup heavy cream
- 2 pounds chicken breast (skinless & boneless)
- Butter

Directions:

1. Cut chicken breast into 1 ½ inch pieces
2. Then blend almond, pepper, garlic and cilantro until smooth, once done, blend the cream. Coat the chicken with this sauce.
3. Preheat grill for 375 degrees F for 30 mins
4. Skewer meat (4 per skewer) and season eat skewer accordingly
5. Brush butter onto skewer
6. Cook chicken on medium heat until done.

Chili Bay Leaf chicken soup

Ingredients:

- 13 oz chicken fillet, cooked
- 4.2 oz celery stalk
- 1 teaspoon salt
- 1 teaspoon chili pepper
- 4 cups chicken stock
- 1 teaspoon paprika
- 2 garlic cloves
- 1 bay leaf
- 1 white onion

- 2 oz white mushrooms

Directions:

1. Preheat the chicken stock in the saucepan.
2. Chop the white mushrooms and add them in the hot chicken stock.
3. Sprinkle the mixture with salt and paprika. Add bay leaf.
4. Chop the celery stalk.
5. Peel the onion and dice it.
6. Slice the garlic cloves and combine them with the chili pepper. Stir the mixture.
7. After this, put the garlic mixture in the chicken stock and continue to cook it on the medium heat for 5 minutes more.
8. Then add diced onion and cook it for 4 minutes more.
9. After this, add a celery stalk and cook the soup for 6 minutes on the medium heat with the closed lid.
10. Meanwhile, shred the cooked chicken fillet.
11. When the soup is cooked – add the shredded chicken to the soup and cook it for 1 minute more.
12. Remove the soup from the heat and leave it for 5 minutes to rest.
13. Ladle it into the serving bowl and serve immediately.

Nutritional value: calories: 167, fat: 6.1g, total carbs: 4.6g, sugars: 2.1g, protein: 22.8g

Onion Chorizo sausages Cabbage soup

Ingredients:

- 10-ounce chorizo sausages
- 10.6 oz white cabbage

- 1 green pepper
- 5 garlic cloves
- 1 teaspoon olive oil
- 1 white onion
- ½ teaspoon ground black pepper
- ½ teaspoon cayenne pepper
- 1 teaspoon salt
- 1 teaspoon cilantro
- ½ teaspoon oregano
- 4 cups water
- 1 teaspoon onion powder

Directions:

1. Slice the chorizo sausages.
2. Preheat the pan and pour olive oil.
3. Toss the sliced chorizo sausages in the pan and cook them for 2 minutes on the medium heat. Stir the sausages frequently.
4. Chop the white cabbage.
5. Remove the seeds from the green pepper and dice it.
6. Peel the garlic cloves and slice them.
7. Peel the onion and dice it.
8. Take the shallow bowl and combine ground black pepper, cayenne pepper, salt, cilantro, oregano, and onion powder. Stir the mixture.
9. Take the mixing bowl and combine the diced onion, sliced garlic cloves and cabbage together. Mix up the mass.
10. Sprinkle the mixture with the spices and stir it gently.
11. Take the saucepan and pour water.
12. Preheat the saucepan on the high heat till it becomes to boil.
13. Then add cabbage mixture and diced green pepper.
14. Cook the soup for 10 minutes on the medium heat.
15. Then add fried chorizo sausages and cook the soup for 10 minutes more on the low heat.
16. When the soup is cooked – remove it from the heat and leave it for at least 5 minutes.
17. Ladle the soup into the serving bowl and serve it immediately.

Yummy Walnuts Beef stew

Ingredients:

- 1-pound beef brisket
- 1 teaspoon rosemary
- 2 cups beef broth
- 1 oz walnuts
- 1 tablespoon mustard
- 1/3 oz flax meal
- 1 teaspoon salt
- 1 teaspoon paprika
- ½ teaspoon ground black pepper
- ¼ cup cream cheese
- 10 oz asparagus
- 7 oz avocado, pitted

Directions:

1. Chop the beef brisket and put the meat in the mixing bowl.
2. Sprinkle the chopped beef with the rosemary, mustard, salt, paprika, and ground black pepper.
3. Stir the mixture carefully with the help of the hands. Leave the mixture.
4. Meanwhile, chop the avocado and cut the asparagus into 4 parts.
5. Crush the walnuts.
6. Pour the beef broth into the saucepan and start to preheat it.
7. When the liquid becomes to boil – add chopped beef brisket and simmer it for 15 minutes on the medium heat.

8.   After this, add asparagus and cream cheese.

9.   Continue to cook the stew for 15 minutes more.

10.   Then combine the chopped avocado and cream cheese together. Stir the mixture.

11.   Sprinkle the mass with the flax meal and stir it gently again.

12.   Transfer the cream cheese mixture in the stew and stir it carefully till you get homogenous mass.

13.   Close the lid and cook the stew for 10 minutes more.

14.   Remove the stew from the heat and sprinkle it with the walnuts.

15.   Serve the dish immediately.

Delicious Bacon and cabbage stew

Ingredients:
- 7 oz bacon strips
- 1 teaspoon salt
- ½ teaspoon nutmeg
- 1 teaspoon turmeric
- 1 teaspoon ground black pepper
- 7 oz white cabbage
- 2 cups bone broth
- 1 tablespoon almond milk
- 1 teaspoon butter
- 2 green peppers

Directions:

1.   Remove the seeds from the green peppers and chop them roughly.

2.   Preheat the skillet on the medium heat and toss butter.

3.   Add chopped green peppers and cook it for 2 minutes on the high heat.

4.   Stir it constantly.

5. Chop the cabbage.

6. Chop the bacon strips roughly.

7. Take the mixing bowl and transfer the chopped cabbage. Sprinkle it with salt and nutmeg. Stir the mixture.

8. Sprinkle the chopped bacon with the turmeric, ground black pepper, and almond milk. Stir it.

9. Take the big saucepan and put the spiced bacon.

10. Add bone broth and cook the dish for 5 minutes.

11. Then add chopped cabbage and green peppers.

12. Stir the mixture.

13. Close the lid and simmer the dish for 15 minutes more.

14. Then mix up the stew and serve it immediately.

Bacon Cheese Stuffed Hot Dogs Wrapped

Ingredients:
- 10 hot dogs
- 20 slices bacon
- 3 ounces cheddar cheese, chopped into small rectangles
- 1 teaspoon garlic powder
- 1 teaspoon onion powder
- Salt to taste
- Pepper to taste

Directions:

1. Slit the hotdogs in the middle leaving the sides intact.

2. Gently insert the cheese pieces inside the slits.

3. Wrap the hot dog tightly with 2 slices of bacon. First place a slice of bacon at one end, insert a toothpick and start wrapping. Place the next slice overlapping the end of the first one. Insert tooth picks on the other end of the hot dog.

4. Sprinkle salt, pepper, onion, and garlic powder.

5. Place on the wire rack of a preheated oven.

6. Bake at 400 degrees F for about 40 minutes or until golden brown.

7. Serve with a creamy spinach dip.

Ginger pork with broccoli

Ingredients

- 2 tablespoons butter
- 1 pound pork chops, sliced into small chunks
- 1 teaspoon kosher salt
- 1 teaspoon garlic powder
- 1 teaspoon ginger powder
- 1 teaspoon onion powder
- 2 tablespoons lemon juice
- ½ teaspoon fish sauce
- ½ teaspoon ground pepper
- 4 cups broccoli florets
- 1 cup coconut aminos
- Some freshly chopped cilantro leaves
- 1 teaspoon red pepper flakes
- Slices of two lemon for garnish

Directions:

1. Melt some butter in a pan over low heat.

2. Combine garlic powder, ginger powder, onion powder, salt and pepper in a bowl.

3. Add the pork chunks to the pan and sprinkle the spice mix on top. Cook the pork for about 3-4 minutes on high flame until it is browned form both sides. Transfer into another bowl.

4. Turn the heat to low and add the coconut aminos to the pan along with some lemon juice and fish sauce. Let this sauce simmer for about 8-9 minutes on medium heat until it is thickened.

5. Steam the broccoli florets in batches over a steamer for about 5minutes. Ensure that you do not over steam the broccoli.

6. Now place the steamed broccoli florets on a large plate. Add the cooked pork chunks over the florets.

7. Now pour the sauce on top.

8. Garnish with some fresh cilantro and lemon slices on top.

9. Serve hot.

Stecia Beef satay

Ingredients:

- 10 oz beef brisket
- 1 teaspoon tamari
- 1 teaspoon stevia
- 1 tablespoon coconut oil
- ½ teaspoon chili paste

Directions:

1. Cut the beef brisket into the strips.

2. Combine stevia and chili paste together and stir the mixture.

3. After this, sprinkle the beef strips with the tamari and mix up mass carefully.

4. Then preheat the skillet and pour coconut oil.
5. Toss the beef strips in the preheated skillet and cook it for 10 minutes on the medium heat.
6. After this, add stevia mixture continue to cook it on the medium heat for 10 minutes more.
7. When the meat is soft – remove it from the skillet and serve it hot.
8. Enjoy!

Garlic Kale with bacon

Ingredients
- 2 large bunches of kale leaves
- 2 cups chopped onions
- 4 cloves garlic
- 6 slices raw bacon
- 4 tbsp. butter

Directions:
1. Take a skillet and place it on a medium flame and add butter to it.
2. Cut the bacon into small strips or pieces and add them to the skillet.
3. Cook the bacon well.
4. Add the onion to the skillet and sauté until it is translucent. Add the garlic to the skillet.
5. Once the garlic and the onions have cooked, add the kale leaves.
6. Sauté on a medium flame and stir occasionally. You have to ensure that you are turning the leaves over to cook them well. This will mix the onion and the bacon well.
7. Cook the kale until it is softened. This may take an hour.

Yummy Asian Spices Barbecued Ribs

Ingredients:

6 short rib flanks
2 tablespoons fish sauce
2 tablespoons coconut aminos
1 tablespoon oyster sauce
2 tablespoons rice vinegar
½ teaspoon red pepper flakes
1 teaspoon minced ginger
1 teaspoon minced garlic
½ teaspoon sesame seeds
½ teaspoon onion powder
1 tablespoon salt

Directions:

Combine the rice vinegar, oyster sauce, fish sauce, and coconut aminos in a large bowl. Place the short ribs in the marinade and let it sit for 1 hour.

In a separate bowl, mix the pepper flakes, ginger, garlic, onion powder, salt, and sesame seeds. Rub the spice mix into the marinated short ribs.

Place the short ribs on the barbecue grill and cook each side for 5 minutes. Remove the meat from the grill and slice into smaller portions. Serve while hot.

Turmeric Spicy beef steak

Ingredients:

- 15 oz beef steak
- 1 tablespoon lemon juice
- 1 tablespoon coconut oil
- 1 tablespoon almond milk
- 1 teaspoon turmeric
- 1 teaspoon basil
- 1 teaspoon oregano
- 1 teaspoon ground black pepper
- 1 teaspoon cilantro
- 1 tablespoon rosemary
- 2 tablespoon butter
- 1teaspoon mustard
- 1 teaspoon apple cider vinegar

Directions:

1. Beat the steaks gently.
2. Take the shallow bowl and combine turmeric, basil, oregano, ground black pepper, cilantro, and rosemary together. Stir the mixture gently.
3. Then sprinkle the meat with the spice mixture and stir it carefully.
4. After this, rub the steaks with the mustard and sprinkle them with the apple cider vinegar.
5. Leave the meat for 5 minutes.
6. Meanwhile, combine the butter, almond milk, and coconut oil together. Stir it.
7. Preheat the skillet well and pour the almond milk mixture.
8. Then transfer the meat to the skillet and cook it for 15 minutes from the both sides on the medium heat.
9. When the meat is soft – remove it from the skillet and serve it hot.

Coconut Asparagus Bacon Wrapped

Ingredients:

- 15 oz asparagus
- 10 oz bacon strips
- 1 teaspoon salt
- 1 tablespoon butter
- 1 teaspoon coconut oil
- ½ teaspoon chili flakes
- 1 teaspoon oregano
- ½ teaspoon turmeric
- 1 cup water

Directions:

1. Wash the asparagus carefully.
2. Steam the asparagus in the water for 5 minutes.
3. Put the bacon strips in the mixing bowl and sprinkle the meat with salt, chili flakes, oregano, and turmeric.
4. Mix up the mass carefully.
5. After this, wrap asparagus in the bacon strips.
6. Preheat the skillet and toss the butter.
7. Add the wrapped asparagus in the skillet and cook it for 8 minutes.
8. Stir it frequently.
9. When the asparagus is cooked – remove it from the skillet, chill it little and sprinkle with the coconut oil.
10. Serve immediately.

Mozzarella Broccoli Turkey Sausage

Ingredients

- 2 tbsp. coconut oil
- ½ lb. ground turkey sausage
- ½ onion
- 2 cloves garlic, minced
- 2 cups small broccoli florets, steamed
- 2 oz. cream cheese, softened
- 6 eggs
- 1 cup shredded mozzarella

Directions:

1. Heat the coconut oil and add the turkey sausage, onions, and garlic. Cook until the turkey is thoroughly browned.
2. Add the broccoli, cream cheese, and six eggs. Stir well and continue cooking over low heat until the mixture starts to firm up.
3. Sprinkle the mozzarella over the top and transfer to the broiler. Cook for 3-4 more minutes until the eggs are firm and the cheese is bubbling. Serve.

Juicy Oregano lamb ribs

Ingredients:

- 17 oz lamb ribs
- 1 tablespoon Stevia

- 1 tablespoon lemon juice
- 2 tablespoon olive oil
- ½ cup chicken stock
- 1 teaspoon ground black pepper
- 1 teaspoon oregano
- 1 teaspoon salt

Directions:

1. Chop the lamb ribs roughly.
2. Transfer the lamb ribs in the mixing bowl and sprinkle it with the ground black pepper, oregano, and salt.
3. Mix up the mixture carefully.
4. After this, combine stevia and lemon juice together. Stir it.
5. Sprinkle the meat with the stevia mixture and stir it carefully again.
6. Preheat the skillet and pour olive oil.
7. Toss the lamb ribs in the preheated skillet and fry them for 2 minutes on the high heat from the both sides.
8. After this, transfer the meat in the pan and pour chicken stock.
9. Close the lid and simmer the ribs for 30 minutes on the medium heat.
10. When the ribs are cooked – remove them from the oven and chill them little.

Soy Sauce Sesame Shrimp Fried 'Rice'

Ingredients

- 2 + 2 tbsp. coconut oil
- 3 cups grated cauliflower

- 2 bell peppers, chopped
- 6 green onions, thinly sliced
- 1 lb. shrimp
- 4 eggs, lightly beaten
- 1 tbsp. soy sauce
- 2 tbsp. toasted sesame oil

Directions:

1. Heat 2 tbsp. of coconut oil in a large skillet over high heat. Add shrimp and cook for 2-4 minutes until opaque and pink. Remove from pan and set aside.
2. Add 2 tbsp. coconut oil and add the cauliflower, peppers, and green onions. Sautee for 4-5 minutes, stirring frequently.
3. Add the eggs and soy sauce to the pan and stir continuously until the eggs are firm. Add the toasted sesame oil and stir, then toss with the shrimp and serve.

Onion Turmeric Keto Chili Dish

Ingredients:

- 10 oz ground beef
- 1 teaspoon paprika
- 1 teaspoon basil
- 1 teaspoon oregano
- 1 teaspoon turmeric
- 1 teaspoon salt
- 2 green peppers
- 1 white onion
- 2 garlic cloves
- 1 tablespoon tomato puree
- ¼ cup chicken stock
- 1 teaspoon coconut oil
- 2 oz Cheddar cheese

Directions:

1. Put the ground beef in the mixing bowl and sprinkle the meat with the paprika, basil, oregano, turmeric, and salt. Stir the mixture carefully.
2. Take the pan and pour coconut oil.
3. Toss the ground beef mixture in the preheated pan and sprinkle it with tomato puree and chicken stock.
4. Cook it for 10 minutes. Stir it frequently.
5. Peel the onion and garlic.
6. Dice the vegetables and add them to the ground meat mixture.
7. After this, add tomato puree and chicken stock.
8. Chop the green peppers and add in the mixture.
9. Grate Cheddar cheese.
10. Add the chopped pepper in the chili mixture. Simmer the dish for 10 minutes with the closed lid.
11. After this, sprinkle the chili with the grated cheese and cook it for 5 minutes more.
12. Stir the mixture carefully and serve it immediately.

Delicious Butter Chicken Skillet

Ingredients:
- 12 oz chicken fillet
- ½ cup spinach
- 1 white onion
- 2 tablespoon coconut oil
- 1 teaspoon salt
- ½ teaspoon ground black pepper
- ¼ teaspoon chili pepper
- 2 tablespoon butter
- 6 oz white mushrooms
- ¼ cup cream cheese
- 1 teaspoon basil
- 1 teaspoon oregano
- 1 teaspoon cilantro

Directions:

1. Cut the chicken fillet into the strips.
2. Transfer the chicken strips in the mixing bowl and sprinkle it with the salt, ground black pepper, chili pepper, basil, oregano, and cilantro. Stir the mixture.
3. Peel the onion and chop it.
4. Slice the white mushrooms.
5. Combine the sliced mushrooms with the cream cheese. Stir the mixture.
6. Preheat the skillet and pour coconut oil.
7. Toss the chicken strips in the skillet and cook it on the medium heat for 10 minutes.
8. Meanwhile, chop the spinach.
9. Combine the chopped spinach and white mushroom mixture together. Stir it.
10. Add the mushroom mixture to the skillet and close the lid.
11. Cook the dish on the medium heat for 15 minutes more.
12. After this, add chopped onion and cook the dish for 5 minutes more.
13. Then stir the cooked dish carefully and transfer it to the serving plates.
14. Serve it.

Yummy Stuffed onion rings

Ingredients:

- 2 big onions
- 1 teaspoon salt
- 7 oz ground chicken
- 6 oz ground beef
- 1 teaspoon paprika
- 1 tablespoon coconut oil
- 2 tablespoon almond flour
- 1 large egg
- 3 tablespoon chicken stock
- 3 tablespoon butter

Directions:

1. Peel onions and slice them into the thick circles.
2. Take the mixing bowl and combine salt, ground chicken, and paprika together.
3. Add egg.
4. Stir the mixture carefully with the help of the hands.
5. Take the tray and cover it with the baking paper.
6. Transfer the onion circles in the tray.
7. Then stuff the onion circles with the meat mixture.
8. Add butter and pour the dish with the chicken stock.
9. After this, sprinkle the onions with the almond flour and coconut oil.
10. Preheat the oven to 370 F and transfer the tray with onions.
11. Cook the dish for 20 minutes.
12. When it is cooked – remove the circles from the oven and chill them little.
13. Serve the dish immediately.

Chapter 5 KETOGENIC DESSERTS

Coconut Raspberry Lemon Popsicles

Ingredients:

- Immersion Blender (Helps to blend the mixture smoothly)
- 100 grams of Raspberries
- ½ Lemon Juice
- ¼ Cup of Coconut Oil
- 1 Cup of Coconut Milk (Carton)
- ¼ Cup of Sour Cream

- ¼ Cup of Heavy Cream
- ½ teaspoon of Guar Gum
- 20 drops of Liquid Stevia

Directions:

1. Add all the ingredients into a container and make sure you use an immersion blender to blend the mixture together
2. Continue blending and add the raspberries into the mixture and mix until smooth
3. Strain the mixture and throw away any leftover raspberry seeds.
4. Pour the mixture into the mold you want and set the popsicles in the freezer overnight or for a minimum time of 2 hours
5. Once frozen, run the mold under hot water ad dislodge the popsicles
6. Serve when you want or store in the fridge for a great snack!

Yummy Butter Orange Truffles

Ingredients:

For the Filling:
2 tablespoons of heavy cream
3 ounces of dark baking chocolate
1 tablespoon of farm butter
1/2 teaspoon of orange extract
2 drops of liquid stevia
2 tablespoons of fine erythritol
Coating:
1 teaspoon of fine erythritol

1 teaspoon of orange zest – prepare just before making up the recipe

2 teaspoons of natural cocoa powder

Directions:

Set your stove to medium-low and set up a double boiler. Melt the chocolate in this while stirring constantly.

Add in the rest of the ingredients for the filling and stir until well-combined. Take off the heat and continue to stir for another few seconds.

Chill in the refrigerator until solid enough to make balls out of. Divide into nine equal portions, and roll into balls.

Coat with the coating and chill for a few hours. Serve cold.

Vanilla Coconut "Ice Cream"

Ingredients:

1/4 cup of good quality cocoa butter

1/4 cup of good quality coconut oil

1 teaspoon of vanilla essence

1 tablespoon of natural coconut (shredded)

12 drops of stevia

Directions:

Set your stove to medium. Mix together everything except for the coconut, and place in a pot on the stove.

Heat until it is all liquid, stirring continuously. Switch off the stove and add the coconut.

Decant the mixture into a silicone tray with twelve compartments, and freeze until completely set. Best served straight out of the freezer.

Double Cream Lemon Cheesecake

Ingredients:

2 ounces of double cream
8 ounces of plain cream cheese (softened)
1 teaspoon of erythritol
1 tablespoon of freshly squeezed lemon juice
1 cup of sour cream
1 tablespoon of vanilla essence

Directions:

Mix everything until well combined, and allow to sit in the refrigerator for at least two hours.
Serve and enjoy

Rasperries Decadent Cheesecake

Ingredients:

2 ounces of double cream
8 ounces of plain cream cheese (softened)
Half a cup of raspberries (mashed up)
2 pieces of very dark chocolate (finely grated)

Directions:

Mix together all the ingredients (except the dark chocolate) until properly combined and leave in the refrigerator for at least two hours to set.

Top with the grated chocolate and serve.

Delicious Cocoa Coconut Brownies

Ingredients:

1 cup cocoa powder
2 teaspoons stevia powder extract
2 large eggs
1 cup almond flour
½ cup shredded coconut
1 teaspoon vanilla
½ teaspoon baking soda
½ cup chopped almonds
½ cup coconut milk
1 cup coconut oil, melted

Directions:

Prepare a square baking pan by brushing it lightly with olive oil. Preheat the oven to 350°F.

Place the baking soda, coconut and almond flour in a mixing bowl and blend thoroughly. In another bowl, whisk together eggs, vanilla, stevia, cocoa powder, coconut milk and coconut oil. Combine both mixtures together then gradually fold in the almonds.

Pour the brownie mixture into the pan and bake in the oven for 30 minutes. Let the brownies cool before slicing it into 9 squares.

Shredded Coconut Chocolate Almond Squares

Ingredients:

120 grams dark chocolate chips
1 cup shredded coconut
1 cup almond flour
3 tablespoons coconut oil
1 ½ cups almond butter
¾ cup coconut sugar

Directions:

Heat the almond butter and 2 tablespoons of the coconut oil in a saucepan over medium-low flame. Once the ingredients have melted, turn off the heat. Fold in the almond flour, coconut sugar and shredded coconut into the saucepan and mix well.

Pour the almond mixture into a square-sized baking pan and set aside.

Heat the chocolate chips and remaining coconut oil in a saucepan over medium flame until the chocolate melts. Mix well.

Pour the melted chocolate mixture on top of the almond mixture, making sure that the top of the dessert is evenly-coated. Refrigerate for 2 hours then slice the dessert into 20 almond squares.

Honey Chocolate Zucchini Brownies

Ingredients:

1 cup gluten free semi-sweet chocolate chips

1 ½ cups shredded zucchini, drained

1 cup almond butter

1 large egg

1 teaspoon cinnamon

1 teaspoon baking soda

½ cup organic honey

Directions:

Preheat the oven to 350°F and lightly grease a 9x9 baking pan.

Combine the zucchini, chocolate chips, egg, almond butter, honey, baking soda and cinnamon in a mixing bowl.

Pour the mixture into the baking pan.

Bake the brownies for 45 minutes. Slice into squares and serve.

Flaxseed Coconut Pudding with Fresh Berries

Ingredients:

2 cups full-fat coconut milk

1 cup fresh strawberries, stems removed

½ cup blueberries

½ tablespoon stevia

½ teaspoon vanilla

3 tablespoons flaxseeds

Directions:

Place the coconut milk, strawberries, mangoes, stevia, vanilla and flaxseeds in a blender and pulse until the ingredients are mixed well.

Pour the mixture into 2 bowls and place it in the freezer for 1 hour. Serve chilled.

Cinnamon Vanilla gelatin cake

Ingredients:

- 1 teaspoon vanilla extract
- 3 tablespoon gelatin powder
- 2 tablespoon stevia extract
- 1 cup cream
- 1 cup almond milk
- 1 teaspoon cinnamon
- 5 tablespoon water

Directions:

1. Combine the cream and almond milk together, stir the mixture and preheat it until warm.
2. Then boil the water and transfer it to the bowl.

3. Add gelatin powder and stir it carefully until gelatin powder is dissolved.
4. After this, add stevia extract and vanilla extract. Stir the mixture thoroughly till you get homogenous mass.
5. After this, pour the gelatin mixture in the warm cream liquid whisk it thoroughly.
6. When you get smooth mass – add cinnamon.
7. Preheat the cream liquid until boiled and remove the liquid from the heat.
8. Chill it little and pour the cream mixture into the silicone mold.
9. Put the silicon form with the cake in the freezer and freeze it for 2 hours.
10. Serve it.

Yummy Almond Coconut Fat Bombs

Ingredients:

2 tablespoons almond butter

1 cup softened cold-pressed coconut oil

3 tablespoons unsweetened cocoa powder

2 tablespoons organic honey

1 teaspoon vanilla

½ teaspoon sea salt

1 cup shredded coconut

Directions:

Place the almond butter, coconut oil, cocoa powder, honey, vanilla and sea salt in a food processor and mix until smooth and creamy.

Form the mixture into 16 candy balls. Roll each ball into the shredded coconut and place on a parchment-lined sheet. Refrigerate the candies for 1 hour then transfer them in an airtight container.

Vanilla Watermelon Creamsicles

Ingredients:

2 cups watermelon chunks, deseeded
1 ¾ cups full-fat coconut milk
1 teaspoon vanilla
1 tablespoon organic honey

Directions:

Puree the watermelon in a food processor and pour it into a bowl, making sure to discard seeds. Place the fruit puree back into the food processor then pour in the honey, vanilla and coconut milk. Process until the mixture becomes smooth and creamy.

Pour the watermelon mixture into 4 molds and place popsicle sticks through the dessert.

Place the popsicles in the freezer for 4-5 hours.

Low-Carb Honey Pumpkin

Ingredients:

1 teaspoon cinnamon

1 cup canned pumpkin puree

½ cup organic honey

1 cup almond butter

1 teaspoon baking soda

1 tablespoon melted coconut oil

1 egg

1 teaspoon vanilla extract

Directions:

Place the pumpkin puree in a mixing bowl. Add in the cinnamon, honey, almond butter, baking soda, coconut oil, egg and vanilla extract. Mix well.

Pour the batter into a square 8x8 baking pan. Bake the dish in a preheated 350°F oven for 30 minutes.

Slice into squares and serve.

Keto ACV blackberry muffins

Ingredients:

- 1 cup almond flour
- 1 teaspoon baking soda
- 1 tablespoon apple cider vinegar
- ½ cup blackberries
- 1 tablespoon stevia extract
- 1 oz dark chocolate

- ½ cup almond milk

Directions:

1. Take the mixing bowl and combine the almond flour and baking soda together. Stir the mixture.
2. After this add dark chocolate.
3. Take the separate bowl and put the blackberries. Mash the berries with the help of the spoon.
4. Combine the mashed berries with the almond milk and stir the mixture until you get homogeneous consistency.
5. Then combine the dry mixture and liquid mixture together. Stir it.
6. Add stevia extract and apple cider vinegar. Mix up the mass till you get a smooth dough.
7. Preheat the oven to 375 F.
8. Take the silicon muffin molds and fill the ½ of every silicon form with the dough.
9. Transfer the muffins to the preheated oven and cook them for 20 minutes.
10. When the dessert is cooked – remove it from the oven and chill little.
11. Then discard the muffins from the silicon forms and serve.

Refreshment Chocolate Butter fluffy pie

Ingredients:
- 1 cup coconut flour
- 1 large egg
- 4 tablespoon butter
- 1 tablespoon almond milk
- 1 teaspoon baking powder
- 1 tablespoon lemon juice

- 1 cup cream cheese
- 4 teaspoon stevia extract
- 1 teaspoon cocoa
- ½ cup cream
- 1 teaspoon Erythritol

Directions:

1. Take the mixing bowl and beat egg. Whisk it carefully. Add Erythritol and almond milk. Stir the mixture.
2. After this, add butter and coconut flour. Sprinkle the mixture with the baking soda.
3. Add the lemon juice.
4. After this, knead the dough.
5. Take the pie form and cover it with the baking paper.
6. Transfer the pie dough in the form and make the shape of the pie.
7. Prick the dough with the help of the fork.
8. Preheat the oven to 370 F and transfer the pie dough in the oven.
9. Cook the pie dough for 12 minutes.
10. Meanwhile, whisk the cream with the hand whisker until you get fluffy mass.
11. Then add cream cheese and continue to whisk it.
12. When you get smooth and soft mass – add stevia extract and cocoa. Stir the mixture carefully.
13. Transfer the mixture to the fridge.
14. Then remove the cooked pie dough from the oven. Chill it well.
15. Place the cocoa cream mixture in the pie dough and leave the pie in the fridge for 10 minutes.
16. Cut it into pieces and serve it.

Icy Watermelon & Cucumber Sorbet

Ingredients:

1 ½ cup diced cucumber meat

4 cups watermelon chunks, deseeded

2 tablespoons lime juice

2 tablespoons Erythritol

1 cup crushed ice

Directions:

Combine the cucumber, watermelon, lime juice, Erythritol and ice in a blender and mix for 15-20 seconds. Pour the mixture into a stainless bowl and freeze for 2 hours.

Take out the sorbet from the freezer and let it stand for 5 minutes. Scoop the sorbet into individual cups and serve.

Yummy Coconut chocolate Donuts

Ingredients:

- 3 eggs
- 1 teaspoon baking soda
- 2 tablespoon lemon juice
- ½ cup almond flour
- ½ cup coconut flour
- ½ cup coconut milk
- 1 tablespoon stevia
- 1 oz dark chocolate
- ½ teaspoon salt
- 3 tablespoon butter

Directions:

1. Take the mixing bowl and combine baking soda, almond flour, and coconut flour together. Stir the mixture.
2. Crush the chocolate and add in the dry mixture.
3. After this, beat the eggs in the separate bowl and whisk them.
4. Add coconut milk and salt. Stir the mixture.
5. Combine the liquid and dry mixture together.

6. Add lemon juice, butter, and stevia together. Knead the smooth dough.
7. Preheat the donut maker and place the dough into the dough maker.
8. Cook the donuts for 5 minutes.
9. Then flip them to another side and cook for 4 minutes more.
10. When the donuts are cooked – remove them from the donut maker gently.
11. Serve the dish immediately.

Vanilla Almond Butter Fudge

Ingredients

- 1 cup of unsweetened almond butter
- 1 cup of coconut oil
- ¼ cup of coconut milk
- 1 tsp. of vanilla extract
- Stevia (to sweeten/to taste)

Directions:

1. Combine the almond butter with coconut oil and melt until soft.
2. Put all the ingredients in a blender.
3. Process until everything is well-blended.
4. Pour the blended mixture into a baking pan.
5. Refrigerate for around 2 to 3 hours or until it sets.
6. Remove from the refrigerator and cut into around 12 pcs.
7. Serve and enjoy immediately.

Favorite Raspberries Coconut grated pie

Ingredients:

- 1 cup almond flour
- ½ cup coconut flour
- 5 tablespoon butter
- 1 egg
- 1 tablespoon stevia extract
- 1 teaspoon Erythritol
- ½ cup raspberries

Directions:

1. Beat the egg in the mixing bowl and add butter.
2. Whisk the mixture till you get smooth and homogenous mass.
3. Add Erythritol coconut flour. Stir it.
4. Add almond flour and knead the non-sticky dough with the help of the hands.
5. Then mash the raspberries and combine them with the stevia extract. Stir the mixture.
6. Separate the dough into 2 parts.
7. Take the tray and cover it with the baking paper.
8. Grate the 1 part of the dough in the tray.
9. Place the raspberry mixture in the grated dough.
10. Then grate the second part of the dough.
11. Preheat the oven to 365 F.
12. Transfer the tray with the grated pie in the oven and cook it for 25-30 minutes.
13. Then remove the pie from the oven and chill it little.
14. Serve it.

Cheesy Creamy Lemon Bars

Ingredients

- 4 oz. of melted butter
- 1 cup of pecans
- 3 oz. of unflavoured powdered gelatine
- 8 oz. of softened cream cheese
- ¼ cup of coconut flour
- 1 Tbsp. of lemon zest
- 2 Tbsp. of fresh lemon juice
- 1 cup of boiling water
- ¼ cup of granular Swerve

Directions:

1. Mix the pecans, melted butter, and coconut flour in a small-sized bowl.
2. Spread the mixture into an 8x8" baking dish or silicone glass. Set aside.
3. Put the gelatine in a medium-sized bowl with boiling water. Stir for around two minutes.
4. Add the rest of the ingredients into the bowl.
5. Thoroughly mix until all the lumps are gone.
6. Pour the mixture over the pecan crust.
7. Refrigerate to set.
8. Divide into 8 individual bars.
9. Best served chilled.

Tasty Dark Chocolate Orange Truffles

Ingredients

For the Ganache
- 3 oz. of baking chocolate, unsweetened
- 2 Tbsp. of heavy cream
- 2 Tbsp. of confectioners Swerve
- ½ tsp. of liquid orange flavor
- 2 drops of stevia glycerite
- 1 Tbsp. of butter

For the Coating
- 2 tsp. of unsweetened cocoa powder
- 1 tsp. of confectioners Swerve
- 1 tsp. of orange zest, fresh

Directions:

1. Melt the chocolate over medium heat setting in a small-sized double boiler, while stirring slowly.
2. Add the butter, Swerve, cream, orange flavor, and stevia to the chocolate. Stir until everything is well-blended.
3. Take out of the heat. Continue to stir for around 10 seconds more.
4. Refrigerate the saucepan for around 1 hour or until the ganache congeals.
5. Use a spoon to scoop the ganache and make 9 balls from the mixture. Do this while wearing plastic gloves to keep the chocolate from sticking to your hands.
6. Create a coating powder by mixing the confectioners Swerve, orange zest and cocoa powder on a plate.
7. Thinly coat the ganache balls by rolling each ball through the coating powder.
8. To achieve the best consistency, refrigerate if the room temperature is over 70° F.

VANILLA CHOCOLATE PEANUT BUTTER FAT BOMBS

Ingredients:

4 tablespoons butter
4 tablespoons coconut oil
4 tablespoons heavy (whipping) cream

2 tablespoons powdered peanut butter, like PB2
2 tablespoons unsweetened cocoa powder
1 teaspoon pure vanilla extract
1 teaspoon stevia, or other sugar substitute

Directions:

To a medium microwaveable bowl, add the butter and coconut oil. Microwave on high in short 10-second intervals until the mixture begins to melt. Once melted, add the heavy cream. Whisk thoroughly to combine.
2.
Mix in the powdered peanut butter, cocoa powder, vanilla, and stevia.
3.
Pour the mixture evenly into an ice cube tray. Freeze for at least 1 hour to solidify, preferably overnight.
4.
Enjoy within 2 hours.

BLUEBERRY CREAM CHEESE BITES

Ingredients:

4 tablespoons butter
¼ cup cream cheese
4 tablespoons coconut oil
4 tablespoons heavy (whipping) cream
¼ cup blueberries, finely chopped
1 teaspoon pure vanilla extract

Directions:

1.
To a medium microwaveable bowl, add the butter, cream cheese, and coconut oil. Microwave on high in short 10-second intervals until the mixture begins to melt. Once melted, add the heavy cream and blueberries.
2.

Transfer the mixture to a blender. Pulse to blend in the blueberries.
3.
Add the vanilla and pulse to combine.
4.
Pour the mixture evenly into an ice cube tray. Freeze for at least 1 hour to solidify, preferably overnight.
5.Treat yourself within 2 hours.

ALMOND MINIATURE CHEESECAKES

Ingredients:

4 tablespoons butter
½ cup almond flour
2 cups cream cheese, at room temperature
¾ cup stevia, or other sugar substitute
1 teaspoon pure vanilla extract
½ teaspoon freshly squeezed lemon juice

Directions:

1.
Preheat the oven to 300°F.
2.
In a medium microwaveable bowl, microwave the butter on high for 20 seconds, or until melted. Add the almond flour to the bowl. Mix to combine.
3.
In a cupcake pan, divide the almond flour crust evenly among the cups. Press the mixture firmly into the bottom of each. Place the pan in the preheated oven. Bake for 10 minutes. Remove from the oven. Set aside.
4.
In a large bowl, mix together the cream cheese, stevia, vanilla, and lemon juice.
5.
Top each crust with an equal amount of the cream cheese batter.
6.
Return the pan to the oven. Bake for 15 minutes.
7.

Increase the heat to 350°F. Bake for 10 minutes more.

8.

Remove from the oven. Cool for 5 minutes.

Tasty Coconut Blueberry Cream Bars

Ingredients

- 1 cup of fresh blueberries
- 8 oz. of butter
- ¾ cup of coconut oil
- 4 oz. of softened cream cheese, softened
- ¼ cup of coconut cream
- ¼ cup of granular Swerve

Directions:

1. Crush the blueberries gently in a small-sized bowl. Pour contents into an 8x8" glass or silicone baking dish.
2. Melt coconut oil and butter in a medium-sized saucepan over medium heat setting.
3. Take the dish away from heat. Allow to cook for around 5 minutes.
4. Put the remaining ingredients in the saucepan. Mix thoroughly using a wooden spoon.
5. Top the blueberries with the mixture. Put them in the freezer to set.
6. Take the saucepan out of the freezer and let it warm up a bit for around 15 minutes.
7. Cut the dish into 20 bars of equal size.
8. Serve and enjoy!

Coconut Choco Balls

Ingredients:

- Walnuts – 1 cup
- Dates – 16, chopped
- Vanilla extract – 1 tsp.
- Cocoa powder – 4 tsp.
- To garnish: shredded coconut

Directions

1. Add walnuts and dates into the bowl.
2. Mix vanilla extract and cocoa powder.
3. Make small balls out of the mixture.
4. Heat the oven to 350 F and place the balls at equal distance into the baking tray.
5. Bake for 20 minutes.
6. When ready, garnish coconut and serve!

Healthy Sugar-free Cupcake

Ingredients:

- Almond flour – ¼ cup
- Cocoa powder – 1 tbsp.
- Baking powder – ¼ tsp.
- Splenda sugar – 3 tbsp.
- Butter – 2 tbsp.
- Water – 1 tbsp.
- Egg – 1

Directions:

1. Add almond flour and cocoa powder into the bowl.
2. Mix baking powder, Splenda sugar, butter, water and egg.
3. Heat the oven to 350 F and pour the mixture into the muffin tin.
4. Bake for 20 minutes.
5. When ready, enjoy the cupcakes!

Lemon Coconut Bombs

Ingredients:

2 ounces cream cheese

4 tablespoons butter

4 tablespoons coconut oil

4 tablespoons heavy (whipping) cream

2 tablespoons freshly squeezed lemon juice

1 teaspoon lemon extract

1 teaspoon stevia, or other sugar substitute

1.

Directions:

To a medium microwaveable bowl, add the cream cheese, butter, and coconut oil. Microwave on high in short 10-second intervals until the mixture begins to melt. Once melted, add the heavy cream. Whisk thoroughly to combine.

2.

Mix in the lemon juice, lemon extract, and stevia.

3.

Pour the mixture evenly into an ice cube tray. Freeze for at least 1 hour to solidify, preferably overnight.

4.

Enjoy within 2 hours.

Tasty White Chocolate Bark Dessert

Ingredients:

1/2 tsp. hemp seed powder

1/3 cup LC-Natural sweet white

2 oz. cacao butter

1 tsp. vanilla powder

1 tsp. pumpkin seeds (toasted)

1 pinch salt

Directions:

1. Melt the butter in a bowl over hot water, and make sure the bowl doesn't touch the water.

2. Mix all ingredients with the butter once it is melted.

3. Pour the mixture into a greased baking dish.

4. All the mixture time to set and firm up.

5. Placing in the freezer will also help speed up the setting process.

Yum, enjoy!

Cinnamon Butter Mug Cake

Ingredients:

4 tbsp. almond flour

7 drops stevia

1/4 tsp. cloves

1/4 tsp. cinnamon

1/4 tsp. vanilla

1/2 tsp. baking powder

1 tbsp. erythritol

2 tbsp. butter

1/4 tsp. cardamom

1/4 tsp. ginger

1 large egg

Directions:

1. Add all ingredients to a mug and mix completely.

2. Microwave on high for 65 to 70 seconds.

3. Tap the mug against and plate and the cake will fall out.

All done and ready to eat!

Vanilla Macadamia Coconut Custard

Ingredients:

1/3 cup macadamia nut butter

1 tsp. liquid stevia

1/3 cup heavy cream

1/3 cup erythritol

1 tsp. vanilla extract

4 large eggs

1 cup coconut milk (unsweetened)

Directions:

1. Preheat your oven to 325· F.

2. Combine all of your ingredients in a bowl. Whisk well to make sure everything is combined.

3. Pour about 1 inch of water into the bottom of a baking dish and place four ramekins in the dish (the water should come about halfway up the sides)

4. Fill the ramekins with your mixture.

5. Bake for about 40 minutes. A knife will come out of the center clean when the custard is cooked.

6. Cool for half an hour. Serve

Splenda Bite Dessert

Ingredients:
- Butter (unsweetened) – ¾ cup
- Splenda sugar – 1 cup
- Eggs – 4
- Heavy cream (low-fat) – ½ cup
- Vanilla – 1 tsp.
- Almond flour – ½ cup
- Coconut flour – ½ cup
- Baking powder – 2 tbsp.

- Salt to taste
- Water – 1 cup

Directions:

1. Add butter and Splenda sugar into the bowl.
2. Mix eggs, heavy cream, vanilla, almond flour, coconut flour, baking powder, water and salt.
3. Heat the oven to 350 F and pour the mixture into the baking tray.
4. Let it bake for 20 minutes.
5. When ready, serve and enjoy!

Coconut Cinnamon Sugar-Free Cheesecake

Ingredients:

- Eggs – 6
- Coconut oil – ½ cup
- Coconut flour – 1/3 cup
- Cocoa powder – 1/3 cup
- Unsweetened Chocolate (melted) – 3 oz.
- Honey – ½ cup
- Vanilla extract – 2 tsp.
- Salt – ½ tsp.
- Baking soda – ½ tsp.
- Cinnamon powder – ½ tsp.

Directions:

1. Add eggs and coconut oil into the bowl.
2. Mix coconut flour, cocoa powder, unsweetened chocolate, honey, vanilla extract, baking soda, cinnamon powder and salt.
3. Heat the oven to 350 F and pour the mixture into the baking tray.
4. Let it bake for 5 minutes.
5. When ready, refrigerate for 20 minutes until it cools.
6. Dress with your favorites and enjoy the cheesecake!

Dark Chocolate Almond Block Dessert

Ingredients:

- Unsweetened coconut – 1 cup
- Almonds – 2 cups
- Almond butter – ½ cup
- Coconut oil – 2/3 cup
- Coconut flour – 1 tbsp.
- Salt – ½ tsp.
- Blackstrap molasses – ½ tbsp.
- Vanilla extract – 1 tbsp.
- Dark chocolate – 3 oz.

Directions:

1. Add unsweetened coconut and almonds into the bowl.
2. Mix almond butter, coconut oil. Coconut flour, salt, blackstrap molasses, vanilla extract and dark chocolate.
3. Heat the oven to 350 F and pour mixture into the baking tray.
4. Bake for 20 minutes.
5. When ready, serve and enjoy!

Chapter 6 CONCLUSION

Thank you again for downloading this book!

If you enjoyed this book, would you be kindly enough to leave a review for this book on Amazon? It'd be greatly appreciated!

Thank you and good luck!

Made in the USA
Middletown, DE
05 June 2017